GROW YOUR
PROFIT$

Hanan Kattan

Hanan Kattan

10% of profits from all Enlightenment companies are
donated to charities focused on women and children
via The Sarif-Kattan Foundation

www.Sarif-KattanFoundation.com

enlightenment press

First edition published worldwide by Enlightenment
Press, London, UK, 2012

www.EBSdigital.com

www.GrowYourProfits.net

www.Enlightenment-Press.com

www.HananKattan.com

ISBN Number: 978-0-9570752-0-7

enlightenment press

A lifetime entrepreneur of Palestinian background, Hanan Kattan co-founded EBS Digital as an online marketing company that gives businesses the tools for outstanding growth. It is the latest addition to her Enlightenment group of companies, which includes film production, film sales, a record label and a publishing arm.

Her aim with EBS Digital was to address the crucial 'third step' in online marketing - converting the extra traffic from higher rankings into actual sales and profits. EBS digital is a Google Agency.

Her previous businesses included creating her own hair care brand, Te Tao, which launched an entirely new category of 'premium mass' holistic hair products which Marie Claire magazine called 'beauty with a conscience.'

She is also the producer of two feature films, The World Unseen and I Can't Think Straight, which have won over 30 awards between them. Her third feature, The House of Tomorrow, was inspired by the TEDxHolyLand conference that Hanan curated with her Israeli partner under her foundation, the Sarif-Kattan Foundation. The film has just completed and she served as producer and co-director alongside her partner Shamim Sarif, an award-winning novelist and director.

Hanan is an entrepreneur, a public speaker and an award winning feature film producer. She holds a BA in Foreign Service from Baylor University, Texas, a Masters in International Relations from the University of San Diego and a Masters in Online Marketing from the University of San Francisco.

She lives in London with Shamim and their two children.

Acknowledgments:

It is a blessing to have amazing friends be part of the wonderful journey of life. I have been fortunate and blessed to share my life with so many enlightened and inspiring people who have touched my life. They are a very rich and diverse group and I am grateful to have known them.

I will start with the lovely women who helped shape my life:

My dearest and oldest friends:
Katherine Priestley, Lisa Tchenguiz, Kristi Tethong, Susan Coll, Sandra Watfa, Alma Fakhre, Lea Porter, Hadia Debs, Shehkar Jah, Antoinette Claessens, Dina Masri, Jessica Barkley, Abbe Lipner, Azi Pahlavi, Rania Atalla, Filwa Mayassi and Carla Moussa.

My very dear and creative ladies of film and music:
Leonie Casanova, Leena Yadav, Joan Chen, Lisa Ray, Sheetal Sheth, Teri Schwartz, Melody Korenbrot, Stefani Deoul, Donna Deitch, Antonia Frering and Maria Furtwangler Burda

My brilliant and lovely ladies of finance:
Mick Lee, Karen Frank, Jennifer Hill, Michelle Bonn and Ellie Patsalos.

My dear and more recent friends:
Conchita Morley, Basma Ali Reza, Dounia Nadar, Simonetta Coronelli, Deborah and Gabriella DiMaggio, Megan and Christine Bense, Kelly Gonda, Jennifer Fox, Shaz Van Zanten, Muna Kattan (Bethlehem), Dalia Fadila, Lakshmi Pratury, Steffi Czerny and Sue James

My TEDxHolyLand ladies:
My amazing TEDxHolyLand partner Liat Aaronson and my "Palestinian Angel" who made our event a reality.

My lovely TED women:
Miriam Twaalfhoven, Sarah Caddick, Marina Kleinwort and Joanne Priestley

Leslie Fennern who is very much missed and will always live in my heart.

And for the wonderful men in my life:

The three amazing godfathers of our boys:
David Pitblado (our wonderful friend who is deeply missed and whose life was such an inspiration) and our dear friends Losel Tethong and Charles Nasser.

And all the other wonderful men:
My dear Jamaican Palestinian cousin Joey Issa, my enlightened friend Aseem Bajaj, and the lovely Mazen Masri, Alaa Khashoggi, Sharif Nadar and Tareq Abu Zayad. Samir Dajani for his unwavering belief and support and I am eternally grateful to Minhaz Manji as without him I would not have met my wife.

Special Thank Yous:
To Laura Posey, Adrian Ulsh, Madelein Otto and Naresh Shahani for their help and support for our learning process.

To my family - the loves of my life:
Ethan and Luca, my brilliant and beautiful two sons, the men of my world, my rocks, my life.

Shamim, my best friend, my talented and brilliant Renaissance wife; without you I would not be who I am today and this book could not have happened.

To my grandfather, Tewfic Kattan, who made everything
a possibility

And to the loves of my life, Shamim, Ethan and Luca
who make everything worthwhile

Contents

Step 2:

Hanan Kattan

INTRODUCTION

Abundance is in how you view the world

Introduction

In life, we all need inspiration and motivation; someone who sets a bar for achievement and gives you a sense of the possibilities that life has. The kind of person we refer to as a role model. If that role model also believes in you, they can help you generate tremendous power from within.

For me, that person was my grandfather, Tewfic Kattan.

From a very young age, as I grew up in Jordan, I spent large amounts of time with him at his home, which was always overflowing with hospitality for family, friends and neighbors. We also made many traditional visits to friends during the special holidays that are such a large part of life in the Middle East.

But the memories that have stayed with me the most through all these years are the times I spent at my grandfather's offices in downtown Amman, joining him on visits to his factories and to his various businesses. During the 1920s, my great-grandfather had a small business in Jordan and, when the manager of that business resigned, my grandfather Tewfic was sent to hire someone new and then return to Bethlehem, where his family was from, and to continue working for the family business in Palestine.

It did not take long for the untried expanses of Jordan to captivate my grandfather's imagination, and he decided to stay in Amman and put his entrepreneurial passion and drive into building a huge range of businesses, ranging from industry and manufacturing to service industries and even to opening the first cinema in Jordan.

As his business empire expanded, he experienced the ups and downs that any of us who have tried to build a business from scratch are more than familiar with. Throughout, his generosity and philanthropy was unprecedented and he gave the same level of respect to a janitor as he would to the wealthiest individuals and to monarchs. He embodied a sense of integrity, humility and honor in all his dealings; fundamentals that created for me a paradigm that meaningful success in business should always be built on these principles. His generosity in handing out gifts, loans (that he rarely requested back) and opportunities to others became the fabric of stories that people still tell me on the occasions that I go back to Amman or to Palestine.

His contribution to the industrial and commercial private sectors of Jordan's economy led King Abdulla I to award him the title of "Pasha" and he became known everywhere he went as "El Basha"

When I was only eight, he would have me sit at the head of the boardroom table to write letters in his office, which stood near the colorful sights and scents of the souk market in Amman, and he would pay me for each letter I wrote. He would also pay me to take documents up and down his office building to the various departments and he would have me sit in on meetings and encourage me to help out during the summer holidays from a very young age. I loved every minute. As I grew older my father objected that women should focus on marriage and children, but my grandfather always spoke of me going into business as a natural occurrence.

He passed away when I was 14 and at my first year in boarding school in Europe, but his spirit remains in the many businesses and families he helped to start and grow.

That concept of growing something from an idea to a flourishing business, while keeping an ethic of service and outstanding value was intriguing and inspiring to me.

Early on, I began to see business as a very creative endeavor that would allow me to express ideas and, ideally, provide something of value for the people who encountered my company. But I was still very young and unsure of how to begin for myself.

Having completed my undergraduate university degree at Baylor University in Texas, my father decided that I should take over the new addition to his company which was a toiletries, hair care, cosmetics and perfume division representing L'Oreal in Jordan. He took me to L'Oreal's offices in Paris for a meeting shortly before I graduated and arranged for me to have a 3 month internship working across all their divisions and products.

So at the age of 21 I found myself living in Paris (quite a change from Waco, Texas), and given the opportunity of a remarkable internship. I was lucky to be fluent in French and the internship gave me exposure to L'Oreal's entire range from their top flight brands all the way to their mass market lines. My universe soon revolved around learning about brands, and how to focus sales and marketing within the various distribution channels. I found a natural affinity to the subject of branding, perhaps because I was fortunate to have grown up in my grandfather's businesses, understanding something about the international brands he represented, from foods to electronics.

I learned that a brand should have its own voice and story, and a vision that is unique. A brand should add extraordinary value to its users through the products and services it offers. And every company, however small, can start to build a brand identity as a base for marketing and growth.

I was put in charge of the cosmetics and toiletries division, as it was considered the small division of the company and none of the managers at my father's company were keen to run it. We had regular visits from the L'Oreal team who were in charge of the region and they taught me further about the importance of market visits, building existing brands, introducing new products and my least favorite - but very essential - aspect; the importance of staying on top of spreadsheets and reports.

My division thrived and by the time I left the family business around 3 years later, I had taken the company from sales of $250,000 to just under $4 million dollars. For various personal reasons, I decided to leave the Middle East and to settle in the West. Friends and family thought it was a big mistake to leave an established family business but I chose the road less travelled - in this case the highways of California.

In San Diego I signed up for a masters degree and on the side, with three friends, I set up a property development company that built rental homes and apartments. For a while, everything looked rosy but California went through a property crash and we ended up losing our entire investment portfolio. Before the crash happened, I moved into one of the units myself one summer to help fill the other new units. Learning to deal with potential tenants and working at managing properties was another invaluable experience.

Once my degree course was complete, I lived in Texas for a summer while trying to figure out what I wanted to do. I suppose I have never been the type to sit quietly and ruminate so while I thought things through I started a variety of smaller businesses including selling Holy Land bibles and mail order clothing. Some of the businesses worked better than others but what they had in common was that they gave me a huge amount of hands-on experience in sales and marketing in a very short time.

I moved back to London some time later to explore banking as I was still not clear on what I wanted to do next. My father, who by this point was probably hoping I would just get married and stop thinking about work at all, was kind enough to use his contacts and arranged for me to have internships with three banks; the grande dame of private banks, Coutts & Co, Jordan International Bank and, what was in those days the Midland Bank. Those three months completely cured me of the notion of pursuing a career in banking.

It seemed clear that entrepreneurship was the one core love that bound together the work and experiences I had loved most. For the next twenty years or so, I focused on building a variety of businesses mainly focused on hair care, skin care and bath and body brands. I began by representing other people's brands and selling them into new markets by finding and appointing distributors, and then I went on to develop my own brands. Along the way, I learned steep lessons about the challenges of building brands from scratch and growing them into a niche that can fit alongside the world-dominating majors.

For brands to be successful in getting their ethos and message across, they need to resonate emotionally with their ideal clients by telling a story they can connect with. As I went through the thrilling and sometimes difficult process of creating my own products, I realized more and more that it hardly matters whether you are long established or whether you are just starting out. Whatever your size, when the story of your brand and what it stands for is clearly communicated to your ideal customers, you engage at a deeper, more genuine level with your prospects.

Of course, you need to know what your brand is about. And as the years passed, I tried to spend a little more of my energy thinking about these concepts, rather than just handling the day to day issues. When you have your own business, there is always something more to do, another fire to fight, a new product to launch, problems to deal with. It never ends.

As a result, and understandably, few of us take time

to step back and truly think about our vision for our businesses, and who we want to make a difference to, and why. We do not often spend time thinking about what we envision for ourselves once our businesses are the successes we desire them to be.

I learned to take time to set goals and review them, not just once a year, but as a regular part of my routine. It's a habit that, once you have it, gives you time and focus to see the ultimate vision and idea or to craft it, if you are not yet sure of it. It applies just as much to the rest of our lives, from health to relationships too - because nobody wants a successful, cash flowing business without someone to share the benefits with, or with so much stress that the enjoyment and fulfillment of life pass us by.

It was with these ideas in my mind that I was casting around for what I wanted to do after a highly successful hair care brand I had created was sold. I had not been ready to sell, but my business partners had been, and so I was in a reflective state of mind, evaluating my future and my contribution. I had built another brand that had modest success but needed a bigger cash infusion to take it to the next level of growth and after almost 20 years in selling, marketing and creating brands, I was considering what the next chapter should be about. My life partner Shamim is a novelist, screenwriter and now a feature film director. Around this time, I was seeing first hand the frustrations she experienced in Hollywood when she optioned a story of unrequited love, only to get a call saying a budget of $15 million dollars was raised but that she had to add love scenes (which slightly ruined the 'unrequited' part). We discussed this and decided that she should walk away from the deal. There was an integrity to her story and her reasons for writing it that we both felt was more important than making a movie at any cost.

Soon after that, Shamim convinced me to produce her feature films. With no experience whatsoever in anything to do with movies, I was purely driven by my desire to have Shamim bring her creative vision to the screen with as little interference as possible. I agreed to at least try. Another amazing learning curve ensued but at the end of it we had produced two feature films back-to-back, The World Unseen and I Can't Think Straight, that ended up winning 23 awards and 11 awards respectively.

The journey of producing films led to the creation of a film sales and distribution company, which then led to the creation of a record label to produce the soundtrack album of I Can't Think Straight and to sign on Leonie Casanova, a very talented singer/songwriter who had a part in one of our films and who created songs for both movies. In both cases, the large distribution companies offered poor terms or no terms for independent movies that didn't have big name casts. I was inspired to see if there was a way for movies like ours to find an audience, without relinquishing all rights and control to the big companies in our market.

So, from movies and music to online marketing? A natural progression, of course!

And, as oblique as it might initially seem, the journey of the films and music led us to the creation of EBS Digital. While working on promoting and marketing our films and music, we ended up on You Tube alone with over 100 million hits from the various videos that were created by ourselves and our fans based on our two films. These were high figures for small independent films and people kept asking us how we had managed to create a big online following. On the social media side, there is no magic formula. But there are certain 'musts' which we'll look at together later in this book. And by taking these certain steps any business can move to create the right conditions for viral marketing to take off.

We also learned a lot about online marketing in general. The core target audience for our movies tended to be younger and very internet aware. So when they searched for our movies and found an illegal upload or some other distribution channel that we didn't control, we would take a hit financially. Search engine optimization and online marketing in general worked incredibly well for us. But, as with social media marketing, we found that the companies who offered instant solutions and quick fixes were often looking to make quick money rather than to build their brand - or any of their customers' brands. Instead we worked hard for four years to find, build and join forces with a team of more than three hundred experts in online marketing. Every member of the team has their own core specialty and they keep up with a world that moves incredibly fast to find and implement the latest and best solutions.

Overall, EBS Digital evolved from a wish to do things differently and to encourage and nurture entrepreneurs and the owners of small and medium-sized businesses and to help them make a mark in a world that often seems dominated by conglomerates. Because if you are reading this book, you know as well as I do from my own experiences and adventures in the business world that smaller enterprises have plenty to offer. They innovate quickly, they are directly in touch with their customer base and they can try ideas that larger businesses might not be willing to risk.

I've always loved being in business for myself. At heart, I am an entrepreneur, as many of you are who were drawn to this book. As human beings we are always in a state of flux. Being inert, in a rut or just going through the motions are not states that any of us associate with living life at the highest level. Sometimes it happens, but none of us are happy when we fall into that.

We are thinking and feeling beings who are either growing and moving forward, or imperceptibly regressing. It doesn't matter how much success we may have achieved already in our finances, our personal relationships or anything else. Part of the excitement of being alive is that we are always becoming aware of the next level that we can go to. Reaching for the next possibilities gives us the drive to wake up energized every morning. Feeling that control over your destiny, having the freedom to make certain choices and guide the course of your own life somehow feels a lot more possible when you are running your own business rather than spending two thirds of your waking hours working for someone else.

Of course, entrepreneurship comes with its own challenges and plenty of moments when you wonder if you made the right choices, had the right idea, or have any chance at all of making your business work.

The purpose of this book is to let you know that your business can succeed where most others do not. But there are certain things you must do, and those items have changed quite radically in the past few years. We live in an internet world. We live in a globalized world where everyone is connected and where conglomerates have incredible reach. But it is also a world where smaller businesses can reach markets and niches that they could not have dreamed of just a few years ago. In a way, the playing field is more level than it has ever been. And my goal in the following chapters is to give you a clear and easy to follow marketing roadmap that, if you follow it, will drastically increase your chances of making your business a passion which fuels your excitement for your working life, and gives you the lifestyle and freedoms you envisioned when you first started out.

What I have tried to set out in the following pages are tools. I hope you feel inspired to use them as a base to brainstorm and decide processes for your own business, because without application, without taking action, nothing new can happen. When you do take action, from a place where you have considered the road you want to travel, magical changes can take place.

Section 1
YOUR SALES PROCESS

Why are the majority of all new businesses gone within 5 years?

Of the minority that do make it, few will ever reach a turnover of $1 million or more.

The single biggest reason is that the majority of business owners do not take the time to come up with a strategic business growth roadmap for their business, or they do not know how to. Entrepreneurs often start with a vision of their business in response to a gap that they notice in the market, or a need that they can fill based on an area that they are passionate about.

Vision is always a good thing, but it is just a start.

By the time most businesses launch, they have their website, their business cards and a stack of other marketing material, ready, designed, created and printed. Few businesses will have taken the time to really think about the customers they want to serve and the benefits they are offering their ideal customers. This is a 'spray and pray' approach to sales and marketing which often results in very little positive return on marketing investment. In fact, marketing becomes a cost rather than an investment.

There are a lot of reasons business owners do not pay as much attention to marketing as they could. Even after a business has built up sufficient income to keep going, there are still plenty of pitfalls that could make it crash. High costs of goods or rent or other operating costs can eat up your margin and profit. Indifferent customer service can stymie repeat business. Or poor cash flow management can leave you scrambling.

The first hair care brand I created was called Te Tao and it brought Chinese herbal therapy benefits for hair to the premium mass market. Against the odds, it competed in the major drug stores and grocery chains against the established big brands. But that success in distribution nearly finished the company, because those retailers paid us sometimes 90 days after delivery, whereas we had to pay our manufacturers for stock after 30 days. In three years we were turning over just under $8 million, but we had a cash flow gap that got larger the faster we grew. There are ways, of course, to deal with every issue from cash flow to bad management. But you won't get to face any of these challenges unless you get your sales and marketing working to flow revenue into your business first.

Sales and revenue are the first steps. One of the key lessons I have learned is the importance of understanding your ideal client's wants and needs, the importance of then innovating your business by focusing on an area that you are passionate about, creating a niche market based on adding extraordinary value to your ideal client and then creating a strategic sales process as a roadmap to work from; and finally creating a marketing strategy that gives you a return on your investment. What that means in a simple to understand format is that:

- Your business must be unique
- Your business must offer extraordinary and exceptional value
- Your marketing must communicate your uniqueness and value to your ideal clients

If you are wondering where the online marketing part of this book starts, the short answer is that the in-depth look at how to build a website that supports your business, how to execute excellent SEO, PPC and social media is all in the next section of this book.

The real answer to where the online marketing starts is that it begins right here, in this section. This section is about:

- Generating more leads
- Qualifying those leads to find your Ideal Clients
- Converting your new found traffic to sales

I can't emphasize enough how much the success of your online marketing depends on taking the time to understand the fundamental process that I will be outlining in this section.

When my partner Shamim and I started our group of businesses under the Enlightenment banner, we learned these basics over a period of years, mostly by trial and error. When we discovered the principles I will be sharing with you here, it changed everything. And it made us all the more determined to create a system by which we could teach and share these foundational building blocks of overall marketing and sales success with every business that worked with us on their online marketing.

Where Do You Start?

It is easy to point out the things we tend to do incorrectly as business owners but how do we negotiate through the choices we have, when we are usually overwhelmed and with few people to advise us when we are lacking time and resources?

Creating a clear and simple roadmap is the process I want to go through with you in this section. Before we begin, I will give you a quick overview. I have broken it into 7 steps that follow naturally on from each other, and if you can aim to set aside even just an hour or two a week to work on each step, you can make enormous strides and I can guarantee that your business, your activity and your revenue will never be the same again.

This process revolutionized the way I looked at marketing, and we immediately wanted to include it as part of our online marketing at EBS Digital. We did that by setting up a members only site which has this entire process in hundreds of hours of videos and resources, as well as hundreds of ready-to-use advertising and marketing templates, and also modules on time management and system implementation. In fact, we put into it everything we could think of that business owners need to make a success of their initial ideas. It works for offline marketing as much as online marketing, but it is so essential in my view that we include free membership to every one of our SEO clients. Those that use it have used it to help boost their conversions from the extra traffic SEO has brought them, and the difference has been incredible in terms of cash flow and revenue.

Here is the process we will cover in this section, which I have tried to simplify for a book format into 7 clear steps:

1. KNOW YOUR IDEAL CLIENT
This involves learning the demographics, and more importantly, the psychographics that drive your ideal client's wants so you know how to market to them

2. UNDERSTAND THEIR DECISION - MAKING PROCESS
Knowing how your ideal clients decide to buy your products or services is key to evolving your offerings as a business and crafting your messaging

3. CHOOSE A NICHE MARKET
Decide what specific problems your ideal clients face that you solve for them and how that helps you specialize your business

4. INNOVATE YOUR BUSINESS
How to provide an outstanding solution to the niche market issues your ideal clients face, and to separate yourself from your competition in the process

5. REFINE YOUR MESSAGING (ELEVATOR PITCH)
How to create an elevator pitch/message that instantly compels your prospects to want to buy what you sell

6. CRAFT YOUR SALES PROCESS
How to understand where the sale itself takes place and how to get to that point easily and logically with a sales process map

7. PERSUASION MARKETING
How to create marketing that is irresistible

Having a sales and marketing process removes the guesswork and uncertainty out of running and growing a business. How often have you lain awake at night - or stayed up late working - wondering if you were making the right decisions in your business? With some thought and a step-by-step plan, growing your business can be a more productive and enjoyable experience that allows you to find the weakest links in your business and to then innovate those areas to become areas of strength.

Every business owner faces unique challenges, crises and issues every week and sometimes daily. It is part of the nature of building a business, striking out into new territory and keeping your products and services current in a fast-changing landscape. Following the roadmap in this section will not take away all your problems, but it will make clear the fundamentals you need for your marketing before you spend too much money on it - namely, who you are targeting and why and how you can reach them.

We offer this entire method and business process to our clients for free as part of the SEO packages that we do for them. It is our way of adding unique value to our clients and to their businesses by introducing them to the above concepts that I will go through now in more detail.

1. Know Your Ideal Client

Your ideal client profile is one of the most vital components you need to have in place when it comes to building a successful business. When you know it, you will be in the best position to build and grow a highly successful business.

The key to a business owner's success is dependent on your ability to generate revenue. Sales and marketing are the only two options you have for doing that. Instead of looking at marketing as a fear-inducing mass of options, the process becomes simple when you focus, not on just attracting more clients but, on attracting your "ideal" clients. That is when your revenue skyrockets, and it can skyrocket by as much as 16 times if you do it well.

If you are already working extremely hard in your business, the idea is not to make you work 16 times harder, but actually to have you work smarter and in fact have more time than ever before to enjoy your family, friends and life.

So what is the definition of an 'ideal client'? How will you know one when you see one? You probably already have some ideal clients in your business:

1. They want what you sell, they don't just need it.

2. They are also passionate about what you sell and feel they couldn't live without it.

3. You get fewer returns and complaints.

4. They will spend more money with you over their lifetime than the average client ever would.

5. They often demand additional products and services from you that they want to buy because they trust you.

6. They send you referrals and unsolicited testimonials.

7. They talk about you to friends and family and on social networking sites.

Take a moment to imagine your business filled with clients like these. Would it have a different level of income? Would your enjoyment of the business be higher? Would you wake up each day with a spring in your step? What would it do to your creativity? And your profits?

When you properly and specifically identify your ideal client you will find that you are working less and earning more.

Identifying your ideal clients also has a major impact on your business long term. Since your ideal clients trust you implicitly, it impacts:

- New product or service development, since you will have your ideal client in mind
- Customer service, since you focus on what matters to your ideal client
- Marketing and sales, since you want to consider their values and issues in your material

So it is not an exaggeration to say that the most productive activity any business owner can undertake early on is to find these ideal clients, give them exactly what they want, build into your business unprecedented and extraordinary value that makes those clients feel compelled to buy from you and then make sure that your business has the ability to communicate that value to your prospects in a targeted way.

Simply put, you can't be all things to all people, and yet the majority of the websites we see reflect businesses that are trying to do exactly that and be everything to everyone. What happens is that they look exactly like their competitors, and since everyone looks the same, prospects automatically default to the business offering the lowest price.

Identifying your ideal client, then innovating your business to serve a niche that speaks to that client is the way to shift your whole business life from the competitive plane (where there is always someone coming up who is cheaper, faster or newer) to the creative plane, where you literally create your own market, which might be smaller and more focused but which will bring you much more revenue.

So how do you find these ideal clients?

We are all familiar with demographics. If you sell directly to consumers (B2C) then demographics are statistical elements that apply to your current clients such as their age, gender, education, marital status, income level, employment status, and so on. If you sell to other businesses (B2B) then the demographics include the size of the company, the turnover, the location and so on. Demographics define the physical characteristics of every human being or company who needs what you sell.

Think about everyone who may need what you sell. Are they mostly men or mostly women? Is there a certain age group or age range that needs your product or service, such as teenagers or retired couples? Are they most likely single, married, divorced or widowed? What is their approximate income level? What postal area do they live in?

This demographic information plays a big role in crafting the right marketing message because marketing to an 18 year old man takes an entirely different message than marketing to a 55 year old woman.

So it's understandable that when developing a client profile, the demographic information is the category all businesses focus on and it is enough for most businesses to start printing leaflets and designing websites and other such marketing tactics based on their perceived demographic profile.

But it is also the single biggest contributor to why most businesses fail within their first couple of years. The demographics are not the keys to your business success; the psychographics are.

Demographics are important, because they help you to recognize your ideal client when you see them. Unfortunately, demographics only identify the available universe of prospects who need what you sell.

But in fact, we now know from our Ideal Client definition above that the prospects you are looking for are those who **want** what you sell. And that is defined not by demographics but by psychographics.

Demographics identify all available people who need what you sell. Identifying your demographics correctly makes up only around 10% of the success equation for your business. The remaining 90% of your success will be determined by how accurately you detail your ideal client's psychographic profile, which simply identifies what it is that they **want**.

Demographics define the physical characteristics of your prospects.

Psychographics are the emotional components that get your prospects to buy what you sell. Prospects buy based on emotion and they justify their purchase with logic.

Prospects may or may not buy what they need but they will always buy what they want.

This 'need' versus 'want' scenario is a very powerful concept for a business owner to understand.

Virtually every decision we ever make as human beings can be traced back to our desire to avoid pain or to gain pleasure. And we are generally much more motivated by the avoidance of pain than the prospect of pleasure.

So when you supply your product or service to your prospects, it is important to think about how their current situation (before they get the benefit of your product) is affecting them personally. What are they finding problematic; what are they frustrated by or worried about? We refer to these issues, whatever they are, as 'hot buttons.'

Think about buying a car. You want to buy a Mercedes. What you need to buy is a metal casing with an engine that will get you from A to B. Any car with a decent engine and reasonable comfort will do the job. But you end up buying a Mercedes, not because you needed it, but because you wanted it. Your decision is driven emotionally, and that holds true for any product or service you buy, even if you don't always recognize the emotional driver upfront.

What we tend to do is make an emotionally driven purchase of something we want, and then justify that purchase with logic. 'I need a Mercedes because I'm on the road so much, I need something safe and comfortable.' Or 'The quality of Mercedes means it lasts much longer than a cheaper car.'

Another example: what if your old computer is running fine, but you see a brand new Mac that's slim, fast and looks stunning and that you really want? You can afford to buy it, but you don't need it, since your current laptop is working just fine. What are the odds that you will buy it?

If you do buy it, it will be based on your emotions, and when your partner or friends ask you why you bought it, you will justify it with logic. You will say things like, 'it has a faster processor', 'it never gets a virus', 'it's easier for me to carry when I travel' and so on.

Prospects buy what they want and not what they need and they buy based on emotions and justify their purchase with logic.

- Wants are emotion-based
- Needs are logic-based.

When creating compelling marketing, you need to tap into your prospects' emotional hot buttons with your marketing messages.

If you focus only on your demographics, then you will be forced to compete on price and not value. Prospects buy value. When they cannot determine the business that offers them the most value, they then default to price. Focusing on your ideal client will help separate your business from everyone else in a similar field.

How Do I Identify My Ideal Client?

Step 1 - Identify your clients' demographics

Start with a tentative list of traits of every human on the planet who may possibly need what you sell. Keep it broad and general for now. If you have clients, look at a typical range of 5 to 10 of your clients and note down demographic traits that are meaningful for your business. You can look at these main areas to start with:

- Age Range - does your product or service cater to a specific age group like young kids, teenagers, baby boomers or retirees?
- Gender - is your product or service used primarily by men, women or both genders?
- Income Range - what income level do you currently serve? The idea is to find the widest group you could possibly serve right now, in income and all other demographic areas.
- Location - is your target customer primarily urban or suburban or rural? Prospects in a big city have very different transport and locational needs than those in the suburbs. Also, which specific region can your business serve? Is it a two mile radius, or the whole world?
- Employment Status/Education - does your product appeal to executives, or those with higher education? Does it need some degree of technical capability?

If you sell to other businesses, the demographics involve:

- Turnover of the business
- Business location(s)
- Number of employees and so on

An example of a B2C business might be a construction company who do renovations and extensions on residential property. Their demographics could be:

Men and Women
Aged 25 to 60
Married or Single or Co-habiting
Homeowners
Household income of $70,000 to $1,000,000
Employed in executive positions or stay at home

It is a wide range, because the demographics cover anyone who could potentially have any building work done on their house.

For a B2B business example, I could give you EBS Digital, our online marketing company as an example. In providing everything for your online requirements from web design and development, as well as search engine optimization and pay per click management, apps creation and so on, our demographics could be almost any business small enough not to have an in house online team, even start ups, since every business needs a website and then every business needs to optimize their website and to have an online marketing strategy to grow their business:

Turnover of 0 to $10,000,000
1 -300 employees
1-20 locations
Any geographic location

Now since our own SEO company and the construction company from our example have good quality features and provide good service, they could start marketing to this very wide universe of prospects immediately.

Most businesses focus on telling their prospects about the features that their business offers, about their great prices, their wonderful service, their incredible range of products, the vast choice and selection that they offer prospects and other such features.

That is one of the biggest mistakes a business can focus on.

Your prospects want to know how the products or service that you offer will benefit them. They only want to know about the features of your products or service in so much as how your business relates to them and to their needs and wants.

By focusing on the features of the business rather than the benefits to its clients, most businesses finish up looking the same and offering the same or similar services to their competition in an already crowded and competitive marketplace.

This does not mean you can never draw attention to the features and achievements that your business has worked hard to create but later in this section, when we look at building messaging that really reaches your prospects, we will also look at how to change the focus from features to benefits.

Businesses that focus on features almost always compete with each other on price while businesses that focus on the benefits their product or service is offering to their ideal clients provide value that allows them to set their own prices because they stand out and differentiate themselves from the rest of the market place.

But how do you make your benefits meaningful? By looking at psychographics.

Psychographics:

Psychographics begin to define your ideal clients' problems, issues, frustrations and fears (commonly called 'hot buttons') so that you know specifically what it is they really want from your product or service.

The psychographics help you determine what your ideal clients **want** and not what they **need**.

For example, at EBS Digital we found that all businesses

need some online marketing help at some point. But some businesses just want help designing a website, while others want to know how they can get more leads and close those leads to sales.

These are the hot buttons, or deeper emotional triggers, that the psychographics help you define. And in each and every specific situation, your prospects have completely different hot buttons.

Your mandate is not to try and deal with all of them, but simply to choose just one of these areas to specialize in and to create your niche market. This way, you begin to separate your business from your competition, and if you select a niche you are interested in or passionate about, you end up enjoying your work a lot more as well.

Psychographics are important because they help you understand the emotions that your prospects experience and it is those emotions that compel them to buy what you sell.

If you have a knee injury that needs surgery, do you go to your general practitioner, or a doctor who does heart surgery? Or do you want a doctor who has done nothing but knee surgery for the past ten years?

Since you are emotionally invested in the pain and injury, you want the expert and the specialist. Today, that is what most prospects want, in every field.

The key to your success as a business owner is knowing the emotional "hot buttons" of your ideal clients. Hot buttons are the compelling problems, fears, frustrations or concerns that your prospects typically feel when they buy what you sell. They are typically descriptive of a painful feeling, like the dread of a root canal, or the fear that an estimate for building work will be higher than you anticipated. Those are hot buttons, and your business needs to identify the ones that it can deal with for clients.

Prospects want to feel special and that a business is catering to them specifically by focusing on their wants and needs.

So if you were running the construction company from

our example, what might your prospects' biggest fears and concerns be? Well, if you have ever had work done on your home you know that people typically have one or more of the following hot buttons:

1. They are worried about going over budget
2. They are fearful that the builder will start another job half way through yours and drag your work for weeks or months longer than agreed.
3. They are fearful that the construction will hide poor workmanship

So if you could set up your construction company with good systems so that you could guarantee that the price you quote is the price they will pay; or if you can guarantee your work for 5 years after completion; or if you promise to stick to your schedule or pay them $100 back for every day you go over - do you think prospects would be lining up to use your services? Do you think they would be willing to pay a little more for good workmanship backed by a guarantee rather than risking a rough ride with someone cheaper? The answer is yes, because you will be marketing to exactly those prospects who want these issues taken away.

As a small business owner, your job is to identify and define the most important hot buttons that top the list for your business - in other words, the top needs and wants that lead clients to your business. While this list varies from business to business, it tends to be quite consistent within the particular industry to which your business belongs.

So as a business owner, your next task is to list out these psychographic components - the 'wants' that your ideal prospects are looking for. This will start to impact your demographics and narrow them down somewhat.

Now, as a builder, you may want to target people who have previously had poor experiences, because they understand emotionally the pain of having had a bad builder who went over time and budget or who left them with a house full of headaches. If you can offer your guarantee to these people, they will be pre-disposed to want to work with you.

You can begin to see why 90% of the success of that profile involves accurately identifying the psychographics of your ideal client.

In some businesses, there is only one major hot button. In others, there may be ten. Some customers may want a low price, others may want great customer service or a cast iron guarantee. Some may be incompatible with each other when it comes to solving them - for instance, the lowest price might not be possible along with outstanding service - but they are all potentially issues for different sets of prospects.

If there are multiple hot buttons, then your task is to select the one that you have a true passion for serving, and make that hot button your niche market. That hot button relates to a particular group of prospects that is your ideal client. If you want a truly solid business that has the foundations to grow, you need to know and understand who your ideal client is.

When you know and understand their psychographics, you also start to understand how to appeal to their emotions. By targeting their hot buttons, your prospects will pay attention to your message, and want to buy what you sell because it solves a major problem, concern or frustration that they have in their lives.

Whatever size your business currently is, you probably do not have cash to waste. Every marketing dollar must generate a positive return on investment. An accurate psychographic profile is the key step in creating a marketing program that generates real financial results by providing the information you need to reach your prospects emotionally.

Once you master this process, you will be able to effectively market your business and to attract as many ideal clients as you want. As with any process, there is a step-by-step approach you need to follow in order to get the results you want, starting with developing your ideal client profile. Without it, you will be selling to anyone who happens to need your product or service. You need to put aside any fear that you might be missing out on selling to everybody, because there are plenty of clients who want what you sell without you attempting to be everything to everyone.

Create a list of hot button issues that you feel apply to your business. And remember that this list should focus on the problems or frustrations your prospects have, and that you can solve for them.

Using EBS Digital as an example, we can theoretically serve millions of small businesses based only on demographics. But if we specialize in helping businesses who have not had good results from their marketing spend before, we can target businesses who already know the value of doing search engine optimization and who want to be sure they will make money doing it.

We can leave out marketing to people who are skeptical about online marketing entirely, or those who prefer to do everything themselves.

Many times in businesses, 80% of your total revenue comes from 20% of your clients. It's a rule that we will look at further into this section. For now, just be aware that those 20% are your ideal clients - they spend more, they love your product or service and they stay with you long term.

What this process aims to do is turn the 20% into the 80%.

2. Understand Your Ideal Clients' Decision-Making Process

Why do your ideal clients buy from you? This is critical to understand as it will enable you to innovate your business and to vastly increase your profits.

Every decision, within and outside of the business world, happens in one of two ways. It is either:

1. an internal desire or
2. an external influence

If you wake up one morning with a terrible toothache, you reach for the computer and the phone and find a dentist who is close by and who will see you straightaway. That is an internal desire. An **internal desire** compels you to take immediate action.

On the other hand, if you wake up and your teeth are fine, it would never occur to you to call a dentist, even though you might know you have been due for a check up for a while.

Now, what if you are working away in your business, and your bookkeeping and your paperwork have become messy. Day after day, you intend to clear it up and make sense of it, but it isn't a priority for you. Then you get a call from the IRS or your local tax authority to say they're coming to audit your books in a week's time. How quickly would you seek out accountants who are close by and know what they are doing? That call from the IRS is an **external influence.** It informed you of a situation and once informed, you were compelled to take action.

All decisions start in one of these two ways through an **internal desire** or an **external influence**. It tends to hold true in our personal lives too. To create a successful business, it is important to understand these influences on your ideal client's decision-making process. Sometimes your product or service naturally serves one or the other. If you are an emergency plumber, most of your clients will come to you as a result of an external influence like a leaking pipe or a breakdown in their heating. If you are a construction company that does home renovations, your clients are generally motivated by an internal desire to improve their home surroundings. Once in a while, you may get a call from someone whose roof has caved in, and that would be an example of external influence.

There are a couple of ways to start uncovering your

clients' psychographics. One place to start is by doing surveys with your current ideal customers and prospects. This could be in the form of a friendly email, or ideally, an anonymous survey that you can send from a host of easy online survey companies like Zoomerang or Survey Monkey. Anonymity might make your clients more open to sharing any issues they currently have with your services. Here are some questions to ask:

- Why do you buy what I sell?
- What do you like most about my business?
- What do you like least?
- Is there any other product or service you would like to see me offer?
- What problems, concerns or frustrations do you have when buying what I sell?
- What one thing would you love to see us do differently?
- What one thing would you like to see us improve?

These are some of the questions you can begin to ask to give you a deeper insight into the wants of your ideal customers.

But if you don't want to canvass your clients, or you are just starting out as a new business, just the process of imagining, discovering and then analyzing the hot buttons of your ideal prospects will give you a very good base from which to understand their decision-making process.

In fact, even if you do survey your current clients, there is immense value in stepping back and putting yourself in their shoes, and then using the flair and imagination of your entrepreneurial spirit to look at their perspective even more deeply than they do.

Steve Jobs was not a fan of customer focus groups when he came up with new products for Apple. He felt that the customer would often be the last person to know what they want, because they are limited in their experiences and imaginations by the choices they already have.

That doesn't mean you have to come up with outlandish ideas and products. What Steve Jobs did exceptionally brilliantly was to understand his customers' psychographics and then pre-empt their decision-making so well that as soon as they saw a new Apple product they knew that they wanted it; even if the day before they had no idea that such a product was even possible.

The questions you want to ask yourself are:

- What's really going through my prospects' minds?
- What are they experiencing emotionally?
- What do they most dislike about dealing with builders/SEO companies/manufacturers (substitute your business here).
- What problems, fears, anxieties, frustrations and concerns are they facing as they try to decide whether or not they will buy my product or service?

You already know that a prospective customer begins their decision-making process because they want to solve a problem, frustration or challenge that has intruded into their busy lives.

You also know that the solution you offer that will help your prospects solve that problem has to be better than the solution that the other businesses in your field offer them. If you and your competitors all offer a similar solution, you will more often than not be competing with each other on price and you will have far less control over your income and cash flow as a result.

The answer is to transform your business so that you offer extraordinary value. It is critical to the success of your business that the solution you come up with is innovative and has exceptional value and we will come up with some ways to help you do that in this section.

For now, though, the process of profiling your ideal client is always the first step. Simply listing the demographics and then psychographics that were outlined above will give you a good start to this next step of defining their decision-making, because it enables you to identify exactly what it is that your ideal clients want from your product or service.

The decision-making process then takes the system a step further so that you know **how** your ideal clients specifically define what they want.

Understanding the decision-making of your ideal client will help you innovate your business in such a way that you will never again compete on price. In fact, when you do this properly, you can actually charge more than most others in your industry because prospects who are emotionally satisfied buy on value, not on price.

This process creates massive value for your business, and in so doing, makes you the obvious choice for your prospects to buy from, sending prospects the message that your business is in a league all of its own.

Once you define what they want, you need to compare that list with your product or service. Does your business give them what they want? Does your product or service offer the solutions that solve your ideal client's problems in an exceptional way? To do this, we're going to use a methodical approach and examine each hot button by asking a few questions:

Firstly, what does that hot button really mean to your ideal client?

And secondly, does your business presently match what they want with an ideal solution?

That second question is important. Many business owners feel they do provide excellent value, service and products. But often, there are several areas where we could improve once we are looking not just for a solution, but an ideal solution.

Remember that we discussed separating your business from the competition. In order to do that, you cannot just give comparable solutions. Instead you need to ask yourself a third question.

What else could my business do that would create an extraordinary solution for my prospects' issues?

Let's go through an example to demonstrate how to do this, that simply needs 3 columns on a sheet of paper, or on a Word document. It should look like this:

My Prospects' Hot Buttons	How Does My Business Currently Solve This?	What COULD I Do To Provide An Outstanding Solution?

Column 1 defines the problem, frustration, fear or concern your ideal client typically faces when they are ready to do business with companies like yours.

Column 2 defines the current solution that your business provides to eliminate that problem forever from their lives.

Column 3 explores potential innovations that can create massive value for your business by first creating massive value for your clients.

As an example, let's go back to our company, EBS Digital. As an online marketing company working in a fast-changing industry, there are a lot of hot buttons for us to consider. Let's look at just three of our clients' hot buttons, though I encourage you to list as many of your own as you can think of:

My Prospects' Hot Buttons	How Does My Business Currently Solve This?	What COULD I Do To Provide An Outstanding Solution?
They don't understand much about SEO and are not sure it's for them		
They've had bad experiences with PPC or SEO and spent a lot of money for little return		
They're overwhelmed with doing their own online marketing but don't want to trust an outsider to know what's best for their business		

In column 2, we would insert what we do that is similar to the way that many SEO companies address these concerns:

My Prospects' Hot Buttons	How Does My Business Currently Solve This?	What COULD I Do To Provide An Outstanding Solution?
They don't understand much about SEO and are not sure it's for them	We produce informative written material to explain the value of SEO and how it works	
They've had bad experiences with PPC or SEO and spent a lot of money for little return	We promise and deliver top rankings that will send clients more traffic so that their leads increase	
They're overwhelmed with doing their own online marketing but don't want to trust an outsider to know what's best for their business	We send monthly reports to clients so they can see progress	

Then in column 3 - what could companies like EBS Digital do to make an innovation that would add immense value while solving these problems more successfully?

My Prospects' Hot Buttons	How Does My Business Currently Solve This?	What COULD I Do To Provide An Outstanding Solution?
They don't understand much about SEO and are not sure it's for them	We produce informative written material to explain the value of SEO and how it works	We could produce videos/webinars that explain all the steps involved in SEO. We could use real life case studies to show potential returns. Or we could write a book which details our methods so prospects can see the value or do it themselves
They've had bad experiences with PPC or SEO and spent a lot of money for little return	We promise and deliver top rankings that will send clients more traffic so that their leads increase	We could help clients convert leads to sales with a free members access site that gives them all the tools they need to define their ideal prospects and learn how to market to them successfully
They're overwhelmed with doing their own online marketing but don't want to trust an outsider to know what's best for their business	We send monthly reports to clients so they can see progress	We could set up an online dashboard where clients could access previous and current reports, milestones and all email correspondence 24/7. We could also give them a dedicated project manager so whether they are building a site, doing SEO or tracking PPC, they will deal with one person who knows them and their business

Now some of these are relatively simple innovations to make that require just a little vision and work. Some, like the member's site, require a lot more work and focus and strategy. And in fact, while we started out fulfilling the first innovation above at Enlightenment, we gradually moved away from educating people who knew very little about online marketing, to focus on prospects who already knew the value of SEO but who wanted someone to do a better job in helping their business make money. That's part of selecting a niche market, which we'll cover shortly.

While you are doing this exercise, the idea is to think of every possible hot button and every possible solution whether or not your business currently addresses them. After that you can narrow your focus to one or two that appeal to you, that you are passionate about, and that will be enjoyable for you to work on implementing. And it is crucial to focus on the ideas that appeal to you, because you want your ideal clients to be ideal for you, not just for you to be ideal for them.

Let's revisit our construction company example. A few of their clients' hot buttons could be:

1. They are worried about going over budget.

2. They are worried that the builder will start another job half way through yours and drag your work for weeks longer than agreed.

3. They're fearful that the construction will hide poor workmanship.

4. They'd like to have someone to turn to for smaller and odd jobs.

Let's assume the construction company from the example is a good company. They are mainly accurate and careful at quoting and then sticking to their budget, they don't take on more jobs than they can handle and they have good workmanship overall.

That is fine, but they are still like quite a few construction companies out there.

So how could they innovate?

1. They could produce a really detailed site survey and quotation and a fully itemized quote so that if issues arise, or the client wants something in addition, the original quote and parameters are clear and can still be met.

2. They can set up a work schedule with week by week work to be done, and send a daily reporting email which outlines the work done that day. They can also collect testimonials that confirm that they stay on time.

3. They can guarantee their work for 5 years and offer to come back to fix anything that falls down or goes wrong, free of charge, within that period.

4. They could have a 'no job too small' policy and be the 'go to' company for everything that could go wrong in your house.

When you are being creative about your innovations, let loose with your imagination. If nobody expects a daily email or online project management from a builder, that is not a good reason not to consider it. The idea is to brainstorm ideas, however off beat they may seem. You are creating a list of ideas, not committing to them right now.

Before committing you will need to check that the idea will create exceptional value and be cost effective and create a good ROI for your business to implement. But for now, just ask 'what if' and write down the various ideas for the potential extraordinary value that you can add. What might seem like an expensive solution now may trigger an idea for a modified version in your mind at a later date.

Begin each of your innovation statements with the words "We could." Do you think many builders (or SEO companies) go through similar exercises? Very few do, and that is why all the builders quoting on a new project compete on price. If you were to come in and promise a 5 year workmanship guarantee and daily reporting, do you think some clients might be willing to pay more for your service?

Not all of them would. There are always going to be people who price shop and who place low cost over every other consideration. But you don't want to attract everyone who needs construction - you like doing good work and you don't want to compete with lower priced builders who take less care in their finish. You want to attract just some of these prospects, those that will pay a premium for the superior work you enjoy doing.

In the end, understanding the demographics, psychographics and then your ideal prospects' decision-making should end in a win-win scenario for you and for them.

3. Choose A Niche Market

Once you have your list of your prospects' hot buttons and your list of every conceivable innovation, it will probably be clear to you that some of those innovations are more suited to your abilities and passions - as well as more feasible - than others.

At this point, it is a good idea to narrow down the hot buttons that your business wants to solve for potential clients. In other words, you begin to specialize in a particular niche. So, our builder might decide that he can offer better communication with daily reports and a long term guarantee for his work - but in doing so, he needs to implement some processes in his back office and ensure a great foreman on site to make those happen. Both of these might not be consistent with solving the fourth hot button - taking on any small job a client wants done. That kind of handyman, smaller income work will take too much time away from the extra services he wants to add to bigger projects, so he could discard that one.

When you select your niche market, you reduce the potential number of clients you will deal with in your business - sometimes quite dramatically.

The way that television has developed is an interesting example. Television shows exist to sell advertising and we used to think of TV as being a way to reach a huge demographic. So why are there now 200 or more channels to choose from, some with relatively few viewers? Because, in terms of advertising revenue, rather than 3 or 4 monolithic channels, those 200 channels are actually 200 niche markets. Investors watch CNBC. Food lovers watch Food Network. Home improvement enthusiasts can watch channels devoted to that niche. So it is much easier for a power drill supplier to advertise his product to the correct niche and segment of the market - or to his ideal clients.

Often, as business owners eager for new clients, we see a reduction in the number of people we are targeting as a downside when, in fact, by being clear on what your prospects want, and knowing what you can provide to influence their decision-making, you position your business in a league of its own.

You are no longer trying to be all things to all people and stuck in a process where you end up as nothing to anyone. Choosing an area of specialization confirms that your business is unique, because your competitors are still doing just that - competing against each other at the same level, while you now have the ability to develop your business around that one core group of prospects that you have selected; a group of people you have a personal passion for wanting to serve and provide value to.

Since you will soon have a business that caters

specifically to what it is that they want, you will now begin to attract a huge number of those prospects within that niche market. You can be reassured that the total number of prospects that exist in any one niche market is far too vast for any one single small business to handle on their own.

As an example closer to home - when we started EBS Digital, it wasn't to add yet another SEO company to a market already flooded with them. It was because my partner and I had experienced the power of internet marketing **when combined with a sales process strategy** like the one you are in the middle of reading about here. Sending more traffic to a business's website is a specialized job but it is a process that can be followed, adjusted and reported on and many companies do a good job of it. But what we realized was that creating more site visitors did not, of itself, mean anything in terms of sales. What made the difference in converting traffic to sales was when the site was well designed, the messaging was targeted to a niche market and the business innovated itself.

That drove us to add the third step to the online marketing equation and to see if we could help provide our clients with the tools to take their profits to the next level as a result. Most online marketing companies already have the first two steps for effective online marketing, which they implement with varying degrees of efficiency:

1. Dominate Your Keywords

2. Drive More Traffic

We made our innovation at EBS Digital by adding the tools for our clients to fulfill the third, and most important, part:

3. Convert Traffic To Sales

To add this amount of value, we narrowed out the

prospects who wanted instant traffic for low volume keywords for a few dollars and we also moved our focus away from prospects who were not convinced of the need for online marketing. We focused instead on businesses that understood the need and power of SEO and online marketing, but that wanted help taking it to the next level of conversions.

In some ways this was a much more difficult proposition to implement than solving any other hot button. We had to ask - how can we possibly collate all those resources and information and make it accessible, and still make it affordable for clients who would normally expect to pay a few thousand dollars a month or more for such a range and variety of expert marketing information? The reason it was worth trying to answer that question is important as you move into deciding which niche to service. For us, it was worth trying to do this because this innovation represented the kind of service and product we are passionate about and that meant something to me as an entrepreneur who had started many businesses, and who had often wished I had this kind of help earlier along the road.

So when you are thinking about which niche market to focus on, here is a recommendation: never make this decision based solely on the amount of revenue you think you can make from a specific niche market. Revenue is important, but it should not be the only factor in your final decision. Your decision should also resonate with your individual passion.

Which niche excites you the most? Which one will have you jumping up out of bed every morning, eager to start the day? Which one will wake you up at night with another great idea?

Passion is the key to selecting your niche market. With it, you will enjoy your business more and serve people with a true and authentic belief in what you do. Your business is a large part of your life and life is so precious that nobody should be sacrificing the every day joy and happiness for a few extra dollars.

As an added bonus, when you follow your passion, money often follows. When you are passionate about what you do, you are constantly thinking up new ways to improve and build upon your business. This in turn attracts more and more ideal clients, and adds additional revenue to your bottom line. Those clients can sense when the company they work with has that passion and care and it is a major reason for them to stay with you.

There is another factor to consider when choosing your niche market and that is to think about whether you have a special advantage to offer one niche or another. Examples could be some form of special training or accreditation or even an innate talent that others in your field do not possess. Past experience, particular suppliers or contacts who give you better prices or unusual products are all also elements that can be useful to consider.

There is a wonderful metaphor that I learned which I want to share with you, which is that you should think of your business as being an **inch wide and a mile deep**.

Wal-Mart does the opposite. It has the resources and budget to be everything to everyone. When you go to Wal-Mart you can buy cheese, luggage, clothes, DVDs and a thousand other things. They think in terms of being an inch deep and a mile wide.

Small business owners do not generally have the same luxury.

And yet, that's exactly what most of us are trained to do - try to be all things to everyone. And as a result, the failure rate is very high for small new businesses.

So select your niche market and feel good about it. When you can tailor that niche so it serves your ideal customers and is exciting for you as well, then you **get** to work on your business rather than **having** to work in your business. You will get along much better with the prospects and clients who are now attracted to your business and they will appreciate you, since you are catering specifically to them and you are passionate about what you do.

Down the line, reciprocity sets in. Your loyal clients begin to refer their family and friends, give you testimonials and ask that you create additional products or services for them to buy. When you select your niche market based on passion, instead of financials, the money will just naturally follow.

Trying to be everything to everyone will provide your business with a large proportion of clients who do not appreciate the value of your product or service, who might not pay you on time and who might not be loyal. These are the clients who feel that you are not offering them anything of value and they will move to the next company that offers them a better price.

There is another upside to selecting your niche market. As your business grows and as you develop a highly targeted group of prospects and clients whose wants are clearer and clearer to you, it becomes much easier to add extra products and services specifically targeted for this ideal group, and much easier to sell them.

So once you have several niche markets listed on your demographic and psychographic profile then you need to narrow it further and to choose one, ideally one that aligns with your true passion.

4. Innovate Your Business

So we have found that if your product or service is not different from that offered by the competition, then the only measure of value left to your prospects is the price - which is why so many businesses end up competing on price. Most business owners look for ways to innovate within their own business's current situation instead of looking at ways to innovate based on what their ideal customers want.

Domino's Pizza is often cited as a case study in dominating an already crowded marketplace. They dominated that market by innovating. They didn't make the best pizza and they didn't build inviting places to sit down and eat. Quite the opposite. Their shopfronts were utilitarian and basic, and the pizza selection was fine, but not unusual. So how did they become such a force? Their big innovation was to deliver hot pizza in 30 minutes or less, or they would give it to you for free.

In one memorable marketing message, they appealed to their niche market of hungry college students who wanted pizza quickly, and gave a compelling guarantee that made their pitch almost irresistible. We'll look more closely at crafting that kind of pitch below.

They created low-cost stores near campuses whenever possible and hired extra delivery drivers to meet their promise. And the business was innovated enough to be an outstanding success.

Most small business owners feel that they do not have marketing expertise and it is costly to hire marketing agencies to come up with creative and innovative ways to communicate their marketing messages and to stand out.

What I hope I am making clear here is that you do not need a marketing degree or the ability to write brilliant tag lines to successfully market your business. All you need to do is take some time to go through this process of defining your ideal client profile, brainstorming their decision-making and innovating your business to meet a niche market. If you do this, you will end up adding value that is obvious to your prospects and obvious to you and it all makes your marketing messages much easier to create and it makes them effective, whether or not you choose to hire someone to polish the concepts for you.

So how exactly do you deeply embed innovations into your business? Once you have identified the one or two hot buttons that you are excited about solving for your prospects, you will have identified your niche market. But there is also an art to innovating so that your innovations are deep-seated and meaningful.

You can always just tell your prospects how you intend to help them. For instance, I can put a message on the EBS Digital website that says that we do things better or differently. But isn't that what almost every business claims? There is a point where the innovations you decide on have to be concrete and implementable enough that your prospects can see for certain that you are different. So in our case, we decided to offer a guided tour inside the members-only website at EBS Digital University so that business owners know what to expect from our value-added SEO services.

In our construction company example, they have decided to offer daily reporting and a guarantee of their workmanship. Should they then advertise that they communicate well and have excellent quality work? That is a little too generic, and it's what everyone, even the poor quality builders, claim in their marketing.

So the next step is to back up your claims with specifics that prove that your claims are actually true, and this is where your business innovations must also be an inch wide and a mile deep.

A good exercise to make sure you are innovating to the level that will create massive change for your business is to step back into the shoes of your prospects and go back to their psychographic fears. Let's take the third one on our builder's list:

'I want to be sure my builder provides good workmanship and stays on schedule'

Let's break that down even further. What does 'good workmanship' mean? It could be 3 further things in the mind of the prospect:

- 'I want the builder to use good quality materials'
- 'I want the builders working on my house to be experienced experts'
- 'I want my house back and ready when you told me

it will be ready.'

Now you can step out of your prospects' shoes and back into your own. Beside each 'I want' statement, write down the solution your business currently provides for each of those situations:

'I want the builder to use good quality materials'

We use top quality materials from certified suppliers

'I want the builders working on my house to be experienced experts'

All our project foremen have 10 years on-the-job experience

'I want my house completed on time'

We are on time 90% of the time.

What do you think? These are good, solid responses that will make sure that you meet your prospects' expectations. The problem is that when you only meet expectations, no one will ever notice your business. You will blend in with all of your competition and you will never build your dream business, attract your dream clients or make them clients for life. To do all that requires a third step which is innovation and providing an exceptional solution.

Returning to our builder example, the first solution was, "We use good quality materials from certified suppliers." That's not a bad solution, but it's not an extraordinary one either.

So what could this builder possibly do to innovate and add value?

What if, when they start the new brickwork, they source a weather-resistant brick that they can guarantee for 20 years? Or if they suggest the newest polypropylene pipes that don't corrode and have a guarantee that is 10 years longer than copper pipes? Do you think prospects might be impressed that you are thinking long term for them?

And for the client's expectation that their builders are experts, what about offering a certificate showing the training and accreditation that their foreman and site managers have, as well as a list of personalized testimonials that mention the site manager by name?

As for the timeline requirement - what if the builder provided a customized folder with a week by week breakdown of how the project would progress, and then emailed that same breakdown daily with the completed tasks checked off for full accountability? Or in the worst case, he could use that list to also flag up any unforeseen problems and suggest a solution, so the communication keeps flowing.

Even better, what if he was so good at timing his jobs that he could offer a 'finish on time' guarantee and pay back $100 a day for every day he went over? That might not be the easiest promise to implement for a construction company, but if it could be done, imagine how many people would line up to work with them.

So, now that our builder has found ways to clarify the innovations and, in the process, has separated himself from all of the competition, the builder can complete this exercise by summarizing the benefits that all of this will ultimately bring to his clients.

If you remember the simple table we used earlier, this just means adding another column to the end - which summarizes the **benefits** your clients would receive if you could provide your outstanding solution:

My Prospects' Hot Buttons	How Does My Business Currently Solve This?	What Could I Do To Provide An Outstanding Solution?	Benefits To My Prospects
I want the builder to use good quality materials	We use top quality materials from certified suppliers	We could use the latest resistant brick and lifetime guaranteed pipes	Peace of mind that their home is built to last
I want the builders working on my house to be experienced experts	All our project foremen have 10 years on-the-job experience	We could provide certification and named testimonials	Creates trust that the experts are taking care of my home
I want my house completed on time	We are on time 90% of the time.	We could provide a detailed schedule, daily reports, and a money back guarantee for every day we run over	They would know that we are very motivated to finish on time and that we are accountable

If you can go through this process for your particular business, it allows you to charge more than your competition and target clients differently. In fact, you will be in the best possible place for a business as you will not be in competition at all, because you will have created a niche for yourself.

The concept of competition inherently carries within it the idea that there is only one, finite pool of prospects in your industry and that everyone is fighting for them. Imagine an apple pie, sliced up. Once all the slices are taken, there are no more and so everyone competes for a piece of that one pie.

Creation as a concept is completely the opposite, and as business owners and indeed, as people, we all thrive much more and offer more value when we are creators rather than competitors. Creating your own niche assures you of a smaller but constant supply of prospects and customers without fighting with your competitors for them.

You are able to rise above that competition primarily because these innovations that you are now creating and implementing in your business are not being done for the sake of innovation but to speak to the specific wants of your ideal clients.

5. Refine Your Messaging

For your business to be successful, it must be and do three things:

1. Be unique
2. Offer extraordinary value
3. Be able to communicate your uniqueness and value

Once you have created your niche market and innovated to offer an extraordinary product or service, you need to create a pitch that emotionally resonates with your ideal client and lets them know what you have been doing to meet their needs in a better way than they have ever been met before.

You have all heard the term 'elevator pitch', which literally refers to a marketing message short enough to use in an elevator when someone asks you 'What do you do?' Sometimes it has a connotation of a message which is super slick that can be a little inauthentic. That inauthenticity can happen when you produce a pitch without taking any time to think about your ideal client, your niche or your innovations.

A good elevator pitch should be an encapsulation of your business's USP, or Unique Selling Proposition, delivered in a natural, conversational way.

When I talk about an elevator pitch, I mean a concise, crafted message that stems naturally from your innovations and the benefits for your ideal prospects. You should always be able to concisely and yet accurately tell people what you do in a way that interests them. This last point is key because the ultimate aim of the elevator pitch is to get prospects to ask you 'How do you do that?'

If that seems daunting, there is a step by step process to creating an emotionally compelling message that acknowledges your ideal customers' wants and needs at every point of the communication process with them, whether you meet them face to face, through your website, via e-mail, your brochure or any online and offline medium that you use to communicate with your ideal clients and prospects.

At the end of this process, you will have a laser-focused marketing message that will engage your core prospects every time rather than a generic spray and pray message that might occasionally have an impact.

Think of it as focusing the sun's rays through a magnifying glass onto a piece of paper. With enough focus you can easily make that light burn through the paper. Without it, the light is scattered everywhere. That's where many small businesses find their marketing messages - scattered amongst every conceivable demographic prospect, rather than laser-focused to ideal prospects who will be easier to convert and much easier to work with.

Most marketing messages that are forgettable or that do not inspire any action focus on highlighting the features of a product or service instead of focusing on the benefits to those who use them.

Prospects want to know about the benefits they will enjoy when they purchase what you sell.

As a result, your marketing message should be focused on creating an emotional response - and the best way to evoke emotion in your prospect is by focusing on what your product or service will do to make their lives much better.

To recap what we discussed about demographics versus psychographics - the reason that psychographics form 90% of your success in marketing is that people buy based on emotional reasons. It can take some looking to find the emotions behind every successful marketing campaign, but they are almost always there. Logical justification might well follow, but your prospects are compelled to engage with you based on emotion.

Telling prospects you offer a large selection, a great service, the best prices or that you have been in business for 10 years, is fine as reassuring background, but ultimately it does not mean a tremendous amount to them and does not emotionally engage them.

There is a context to consider here. We are all completely saturated with marketing messages. From the moment we wake up, whether you pick up a newspaper, turn on the TV or radio, or go online to surf or check email, there is an almost constant assault of advertising messages coming at you. Food packaging, corporate waiting rooms, sports events and even the athletes who take part in sports events, are covered in ads.

And how much attention do we pay to these as a result? You probably filter out most of them from your conscious thought all day. Unless one of them hits a hot button that means something to you.

If you are dreading having your house filled with builders and dust, would a message that offered you money for every day they went over budget catch your attention? Beyond a shadow of a doubt, it would.

The good news is that because you have already put the time and effort into investigating exactly who your prospects are, what they want most and how your business can uniquely meet that want, your marketing message stands an excellent chance of interrupting your ideal prospects and sending them to your business for more information, if not for an immediate sale.

So, your marketing message should stay focused on the benefits you provide and, using those benefits as a starting point, you need to create your elevator pitch - a line or two that will emotionally resonate with your ideal clients.

When your ideal prospects encounter your marketing message, whether in the form of an elevator pitch, an advert headline or the message on your website, it should aim to:

1. Interrupt them in the middle of their busy lives
2. Engage them enough that they want to know more and take action to find out more

If you haven't yet taken some time to develop your ideal client profile using the steps above, I would suggest doing so, all the way through to deciding your niche market, deciding on your innovations and then writing out that fourth column, which outlines the benefits to your prospects and clients from your innovations and new specializations.

Only based on all of this should you then create your elevator pitch. If that sounds like more work than you want to take on, I can tell you that it can be a matter of a few hours spread over a few weeks to do this process and when you see the new potential for your business to innovate, you will get excited about it.

It is also worth it because the end result is not just an elevator pitch that you can use when you meet people. Once your elevator pitch is created and tested, you can adapt and roll it into all of your marketing and advertising materials. This elevator pitch should form the absolute core of your business's marketing.

When you attend a social or a business function and someone asks you what you do, have you ever replied 'I'm a consultant' or 'I'm in construction' or 'I run an online marketing company? 99% of us have done that and most of us still do.

There's nothing inherently wrong with that approach but it certainly does not compel anyone to ask more. Often people do ask more, but wouldn't it be a good feeling to know they were asking because they were genuinely intrigued rather than just being polite?

Crafting Your Elevator Pitch

Since condensing all your prospect's hot buttons, along with your innovative solutions and the benefits to them can be a little daunting to begin with, try starting with a 1 minute pitch that covers the full extent of what you've learned. From there it becomes easier to reduce it down, and as a bonus, you will end up with different lengths of messaging that you can use in a number of different situations and across a range of marketing materials.

Let's start with a series of phrases which will begin the process and after each one you more or less fill in the blanks with the work you've already done in this section.

Start with the phrase:

'I work with' (this could be 'we' if that's more appropriate for you). Then insert the appropriate entries from your ideal client profile. Next, you can say:

'who struggle with' and you insert the most deeply felt problems, fears and issues that most clients face in your industry - and these are generally exactly the hot buttons you identified when you ran through your clients' decision-making process. Then comes:

'and would like to.' Here you insert the innovations you have come up with. The next phrase is:

'What makes my (insert your product/service)

different from...' Here you would fill in 'other builders' or something similar. You can name specific companies in your field, but there is a chance that naming competitors can create a sense of competition, and you don't need to compete, since you have created a new niche. And the follow up phrase is:

'is that we or I...' Here you insert your unique selling proposition (which we will develop by the end of this section). The template finishes with a bold claim or offer:

'As a result, my clients receive...' and you can fill in what the benefits are for those who receive your outstanding service.

Let's try it with the construction company example:

'**I work with** homeowners who want a larger, exceptional living space, but **who worry about** builders who are always over budget, have poor workmanship and who take forever to finish, and they would like to find a builder who is highly experienced, guarantees their work and finishes on time, every time. **What makes my company different** from many of the other construction companies in this area **is that I** give a long term guarantee on my materials, a 5 years guarantee on all my workmanship and I pay my clients $100 a day for every day that I run over time. **As a result, my clients** don't have to suffer to get the home of their dreams, they can enjoy the process and feel secure that we take full accountability for any future problems.'

Let me ask you a question. If you were even considering doing building work to your home, and you heard someone say this to you, would you not ask 'How do you do that?' Most likely you would immediately book him to come and give you a quotation.

As another example; this might be a longer elevator

pitch I could use when talking about EBS Digital:

'**We work with** companies who want to use online marketing to increase their revenue but **who are tired of** spending money and getting poor returns. **What makes our company different** from many other SEO companies **is that we** not only use a team of 300 experts to drive your ideal prospects to your site, but we also give you literally many thousands of dollars of marketing training and tools absolutely free to ensure you convert those prospects to paying customers.

As a result our clients turn their online marketing costs into an investment that they can track 24/7 with their own account manager and project management system.'

That is the end result you are aiming for. You begin with a message that interrupts your ideal prospects and you instantly go on to engage your prospects enough to talk to you more about your product or service. Then you can provide additional compelling information and begin to establish a relationship.

This type of elevator pitch is about a minute long, and it works well in most networking or social events and you can use it to begin to build your marketing messages.

As a next step, we want to trim this to a sharp, 30 second pitch that paints an instant picture in your prospect's head, and it should be an irresistible picture. I have produced three feature films in the past few years and there is an old Hollywood saying about writing a top quality, three act screenplay for a film:

In Act 1, make sure your hero is stuck up a tree
In Act 2, throw rocks at him while he's still stuck there
In Act 3, get him down from the tree

I didn't produce action films, but the idea is the same for the most character-driven piece or for a romantic comedy or a thriller. People love a story, and they love to feel part of a journey. Your business and its innovations can take people on a journey in which they are the heroes who have a problem and your business is the one that can help them get down from their tree.

As you might infer, the easiest way to create this 30 second story is to define the problem and then the solution.

The problem part starts with:

'**Do you know how..?**' At which point you can describe the hot button problems your prospects and customers face that lead them to a company like yours.

Then comes the solution, which begins with '**What I do is**...' and then you can explain how your product or service solves your customer's problem, along with all the positive benefits and good feelings they get from the solutions you provide them.

So our builder may say:

'**Do you know** how when you have building work done, it always costs more and takes a lot longer than you first thought?'

The prospect of course agrees. She's probably still recovering from her attic conversion ten years ago. Even if she hasn't had building work done before, she's heard her friends complain about their builders, and she can imagine the nightmare.

Using the opener of "Do you know how" helps a lot, because those words put the two of you on the same side of the fence. In storytelling, in movies and in marketing, you want the person you are speaking with to identify with you and the problem you are outlining.

So now that you have painted a vivid picture of a universal problem, you can solve it elegantly for your prospect:

'**What we do is** guarantee our work and materials for

at least 5 years and we pay you for every day we run over - so you can schedule your own time and know that you'll have your home on time and on budget'

There are many more examples as part of our membership site at www.ebsdigitaluniversity.com but for now, let's look at how we could use the 30 second pitch for EBS Digital:

'**You know how** you spend a lot of money on your online marketing but don't always get the results from your SEO and PPC that you wanted?'
'**What we do** is put your business on page 1 of Google, drive traffic to your site and then give you, free of charge, all the tools to actually convert that traffic into paying customers.'

A side benefit to you of creating and using a well-crafted, targeted message like this is that it qualifies your prospects. By that I mean that it instantly attracts those prospects who would be ideal for your business, and filters out those for whom your value proposition doesn't hold much appeal. Those are not the clients you want to take on in any event.

Creating Your USP

Your USP is your core message, distilled from everything you have created for the longer messages above. The benefits of having a crisp and clear Unique Selling Proposition are:

1. It attracts (and qualifies) your ideal customers.

2. By attracting your ideal customers, you inevitably increase your revenue and profits.
3. It acts as a mission statement for your staff and managers and for you, focusing everyone on the core

values of the company and the core benefits you aim to provide to those who work with you.

4. It gives you the basis of all your marketing and creates a central theme around which you can build your online and offline marketing materials as well as press releases, articles and blogs.

So let's return to our builder example. What might his USP come down to?

'Guaranteed workmanship, guaranteed materials, guaranteed on time - or we'll pay you.'

For EBS Digital, a good USP might be:

'More Leads, More Clients, More Revenue'

Both of these USPs could be refined and developed in many different ways, but you get the idea.

I hope you are convinced that spending hours, days or even weeks developing and then refining your elevator pitch and USP is worth the effort. Putting time into exercises like this is time spent working on your business, rather than just working in your business and moving from managing one crisis to the next, which is a cycle we all sometimes fall into.

Once you have crafted a message that you are happy with, it is a wonderful feeling to have control over your marketing. You can also test how well these messages are working for you on your website or through your pay per click ads because one of the immense powers of the internet is the depth of metrics and measuring that it allows - and we will go into that in more detail in the next section on online marketing.

But with or without testing, it is always good to revisit your pitch and overall messaging again and again and again over time, because there will always be a new and better way to get your message out to your ideal client -

because that client profile might evolve, your products or services may change, and for certain, the mode or methods of delivering messaging will continue to change very quickly, particularly online.

6. Craft Your Sales Process

The sales process is your road map to ultimate success.

The term 'sales process' can mean a host of different things to different businesses. I am using it here to refer to a roadmap that guides both your sales and marketing strategy. It lays out a step-by-step action plan that takes into account every possible variable that could occur as you communicate with your prospects to offer them what you have to sell.

The Sales Process is made up of Lead Generation, Lead Qualification and Lead Conversion.

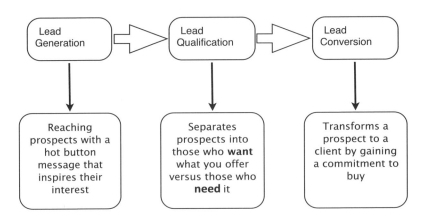

We've already had a glimpse of how figuring out your ideal client and how they make decisions helps you to create extraordinary solutions within your business. Those points of difference in turn lead to benefits that form the foundation of the kind of marketing messages that can cut through the noise that we are all accustomed to, and make your ideal prospects notice and respond to you.

However, where you place those messages and how you place them, is the next step to ensure that they work successfully to bring actual sales revenue to your business. There is no point in spending money on marketing tactics such as print ads, brochures or a website until you know that these tactics are going to help you close a sale.

A majority of business owners do not think about their sales process early on, and instead they produce cards and brochures, take out advertisements and so on without considering whether these channels are the most likely places to find their ideal clients.

Online marketing is all about laser-targeting key words that are based on your analysis of your ideal customers' desires. To ensure that your marketing plan is successful, you need to create a specific marketing strategy which should have:

1. An end goal that you have defined based on volume of sales, or number of clients or something similarly tangible.

2. A detailed road map that defines each and every step that you need to generate a lead, to qualify that lead and then to convert that lead into a paying client.

If that sounds like a clear process, it is, but your job in this section is to understand where and at what point your ideal prospects will agree to a close. Once you have that information in mind, you can create a carefully planned strategy around that knowledge and build your road map and sales process around it.

Do not be tempted to skim over this because you are already converting a certain number of leads regularly with your current methods. You could probably be converting more. The sales process is the reason most businesses fail or the reason that they fail to thrive and grow, because when you spend money on SEO or other methods to generate leads using your ideal client messaging, you must have a solid system in place - a sales process - to deal with those qualified leads.

When a strategic action plan is executed properly it helps you:

- Identify the best distribution channels for communicating your message directly to your ideal clients
- Determine the strategies and tactics you need to effectively deliver that message
- Know how effective your message will be in conveying the benefits of your business
- Be cost-effective and yet highly productive

Distribution Channels:

In terms of the sales process, start by asking yourself where the actual sale of your product or service takes place.

There are 7 possible places that a sale can take place and these are the 7 major distribution channels. Based on your ideal distribution channels you can refine your communication strategy for your lead generation:

The 7 Distribution Channels

- Direct sales - in person
- Retail - in a bricks and mortar shop or some other physical location

- Online - transactions made and completed on the internet via your website or someone else's website
- Mail order - via orders from a catalogue or other printed material
- Events - sales made at seminars, trade shows and so on
- Sales agents - where you have reps selling your products or your services
- Phone sales - could refer to inbound sales made when clients call you to place an order or they could refer to outbound telemarketing to leads, or cold calls to prospects

You need to determine which channels work best for your business currently, and if any others could work for your business.

You can probably see that of all these distribution channels only a few, and sometimes only one, will apply to any particular business. For instance, for the builder in our example, mail order, online, events and retail would not apply, and probably sales agents would not apply either. The majority of sales will probably happen directly, when the builder is on site with the client discussing a quote, or possibly by means of a call from the client when they have had time to think about the quotation.

Marketing Strategies:

Once you have decided your distribution channels, the next step is to look at marketing strategies as the way to drive your ideal prospects to your distribution channels.

Marketing strategies are the approaches you take to actually generate the leads that will end up in your final distribution channels where you close the sale. There are around 20 marketing strategies to choose from.

Marketing Strategies
Advertising (TV, Radio, Print)
Affiliate Programs and JV Partnerships
Catalogs
Continuity Programs
Cross Promotions
Database Marketing
Direct Mail
Directories
Innovation
Interactive Media
Internet (including online ads)
Loyalty Programs
Outdoor Media
Point of Purchase
Point of Sale
Place-based Media
Promotions
Public Relations
Referrals
Signage

It may feel a little overwhelming, but you can begin by checking off the ones that you know apply to your business (or that could apply). By layering your sales strategies onto your distribution channels, you begin to determine the best fit for your business.

This process does require time and attention to detail as you consider each of the marketing strategies to see if each one could possibly or potentially move your ideal prospects into your distribution channels.

For our example of the construction company; as they make most of their sales in person and a few over the phone, a few different marketing strategies might apply. The construction company could advertise locally by printing postcards, or taking a local magazine ad. Those are slightly less targeted strategies, though his headline and USP would certainly catch the eye of anyone considering building work. Referrals would be a good source of leads for him, as would signage outside the properties he currently works on. A website optimized for several carefully targeted keywords would also be an asset. But strategies like database marketing, point of sale promotions or general promotions would not be obvious places to start. Affiliate programs are also unlikely, although he could consider a carefully chosen joint venture with suppliers who might recommend him in exchange for his business with them.

But let's assume he chooses to use just referrals, signage and the internet for now, as his marketing strategies.

Marketing Tactics

Now that you've narrowed the field to a few strategies, the next step is to work on finding the tactics that will coexist with these strategies to effectively (and cost-effectively) generate qualified leads.

The marketing tactics are responsible for making your marketing strategies work. Tactics vary from using SEO to optimize your website, to doing a PPC campaign, setting up a landing page and so on. Tactics do not generate revenues. Having a strategy, and a sales process that is executed in the right order, will generate revenues.

Tactics are the logical steps that you take to execute your strategy. If marketing strategies are the approaches, then tactics are the actual tools used to help you generate the leads that will produce the sales you want. Again, only a handful will be appropriate, which is good news as there are almost 80 tactics that you can use.

Examples of tactics include online marketing services like SEO and PPC, as well as testimonials and endorsements. Printed postcards, network marketing, money-back guarantees, website pages and directory listings are all tactics - so you can see the immense variety and the level of detail.

So how do you know which are the right ones? You need to spend the time to map out your process - the route by which a prospect becomes a customer.

Try to break down your sales process into a step-by-step format so that you can see your specific points of contact with your clients. By knowing these, you can decide the effectiveness of your marketing messages in convincing your ideal client to buy what you sell.

Let's look at the example of an internet strategy, using an optimized website landing page as the tactic for our builder to find more leads.

He would start off by creating a website landing page, following the guidelines in our next section about creating a page that is effective in gathering leads.

He already has a very good USP to use as his headline, and he can follow up with a variation on his 30 second pitch as part of the content.

He can send prospects to that page through careful keyword selection and an SEO campaign or a Pay Per Click campaign if he wishes.

Once the prospects find the landing page, the builder might give them the option to download a free report titled '10 Questions You Must Always Ask A Builder Before

He Starts Remodeling Your Home'

If they choose to download the report, our builder gets the email details of the prospects in exchange and he can then place the prospects into a drip campaign (also known as a lead nurturing campaign) that will give prospects weekly emails with information and tips that position the builder as an expert in his field.

He can also use a Free Estimate button as a way for prospects to contact him, as well as having his email and phone number prominently displayed on his site.

So mapping this process is not difficult - it just takes time, and as you do it, you will come up with ideas (like the free report) that make the tactic even more likely to work.

Overall, the idea of building up a sales process is to work backwards from your ideal outcome and then to put together a strategy to enable you to achieve your desired results. By mapping out your strategy, you remove all the guesswork as to which tactics are best to use for your business. Guessing is what gives a business owner that 'pit in the stomach' feeling in the middle of the night when you wake up feeling out of control, or unsure if you are pursuing the right strategies. This process is designed to eliminate that guessing and to put you on a path that works. It may need amending or finessing or it may occasionally turn out to be just plain wrong, but mapping it out, thinking it through and working diligently on your sales process means that you have control of that process.

To summarize the benefits: having a clear sales process will help you to work smarter instead of harder and to achieve more in less time.

If you don't do this exercise, you will be like most businesses that start with a few tactics, then a strategy or two and who are then surprised to find that no prospects are coming to their distribution channels to buy their products or service. Having a clear marketing program also stops you from spending marketing dollars on tactics that are unlikely to succeed, or at least caps your spend when you do decide to try something unusual.

Tactics are there to support specific marketing strategies that then should lead to a specific distribution channel. Tactics are supposed to help sell your products and services. They are not there to lead your marketing. An example would be sending one or two random emails to a list of prospects, without a planned strategy or vision of how you want to progress them through your sales process and out the other side as paying customers. For marketing to work, it needs to be based on a long term vision - in itself, that approach also builds confidence, trust and rapport with people who are considering doing business with you.

To summarize the distribution channels, marketing strategies and tactics by using a metaphor that is related to our builder:

Completing a finished house is the **distribution channel,** or the desired final result.

Building a kitchen, a bathroom, a garage and all the components of that house are the **marketing strategies,** needed to get to the final result.

Laying the foundations, running the electric wires and the plumbing are the **tactics**, or the basic building blocks that lead to the rooms (the marketing strategies), which then lead to the finished house (the distribution channel).

The Pareto Principle

As a general rule of thumb in most businesses, 20% of your clients are your ideal clients and they give you 80% of your business's revenue.

The Pareto principle was named after the Italian economist Vilfredo Pareto, who observed that 80% of the land in Italy was owned by 20% of the population. This was in 1906. He further developed the principle by observing that 20% of the pea pods in his garden contained 80% of the peas.

This '80/20 rule' applies to an extraordinary number of situations in our everyday lives, not just in our businesses.

Most people on a daily basis use 20% of the things they have. Think about your closet. How many of your clothes do you wear every few days? For most people, it is around 20%. Look at the items in your bathroom cabinet. The likelihood is that 80% of the toiletries or medicines in there are ones you rarely or never use.

Your business is very likely to be similar in that approximately 20% of your clients produce approximately 80% of your business' total revenue.

That 20% are your ideal clients. What would happen if you could attract more ideal clients, just like the ones that make up that 20%? What impact would that have on your income? Your lifestyle? Your freedom?

What if you just changed that percentage slightly, from 20% to just 40%. For the business owner willing to put in the time and effort to identify their ideal client, they could easily end up working less and making much more money - up to 16 times more.

This can happen by attracting more of your ideal clients, but the way to make the Pareto Principle really work for you is to analyze your products and services and find out:

- What do you sell the most of?
- How much do you make from each product or service?
- What is the time and effort involved in providing each product or service?
- What is the profit margin for each one?

This last metric - profit margin - is key. Often a business owner leads by marketing high volume, low margin products. Take a look at how many sales you average per month and then find out the average sale price and income on the best sellers versus the average price and income of the higher margin items

Calculate your total revenue for the month and look at how much time you spend with clients when you sell them your higher margin items versus the clients buying higher volume items. All clients want to be educated about the value they are receiving. Does it take you the same amount of time to explain the value of both the high selling, low margin items and the lower selling, high margin items?

When the time spent is roughly identical then you can easily compare the relative revenue generated from both.

For instance, let's assume our builder does a fair number of painting and decorating jobs, and he also has a reputation for bathroom installations, so he does some of those as well. Both types of work tend to take around 10 days to complete, but the average painting job on a house brings him $2,000 profit while a bathroom brings him an average of $8,000 profit per job.

His team is doing 2 bathrooms per month at $8,000, giving him $16,000 revenue. And his group of painters is getting through 6 painting jobs monthly producing another $12,000 per month.

If our builder could change his marketing approach to target people wanting bathrooms, and generate enough interest to entirely replace his painting jobs, then he would still be spending about the same amount of his time selling, about the same on salaries and the same time per job. But there would be a significant change in his revenue.

If he could replace the 6 painting jobs which created $2000 each, with 6 bathroom remodels producing $8,000 each, he would generate an extra $48,000 from bathroom fittings versus the $12,000 he was getting from the painting jobs.

Previous Revenue Model:

Type of Work	Number of Jobs	Revenue Per Job	Total Revenue
Painting	6	US$2,000	US$12,000
Bathrooms	2	US$8,000	US$16,000

TOTAL REVENUE PER MONTH = **$28,000**

New Revenue Model:

Type of Work	Number of Jobs	Revenue Per Job	Total Revenue
Painting	0	0	0
Bathrooms	8	US$8,000	US$64,000

TOTAL REVENUE PER MONTH = **$64,000**

Our builder has not increased his overheads, or the time spent by his crews at work. But he has made a massive increase in his revenue, more than doubling it. And because he now does so many bathrooms, he is in a good position to negotiate great deals with suppliers and to pass those on to his happy customers, gaining even more trust and referrals as a result.

That is the power of Pareto's Law. Most small business owners today are only attracting on average about 20% of their ideal clients, and yet these are the most profitable.

Now if the builder replaced all the bathroom and paint jobs with 4 full home extension projects per month, each of which brought him in $100,000 in revenue, he would now have an income of $400,000 instead of the original $28,000. In this case, making the sale might take more effort, and he might incur more overheads, but he would have to close a sale only 4 times (for 4 extension jobs) versus closing 8 smaller projects, and if he enjoys the process of transforming an entire house more than just fitting a bathroom, he will be more passionate about it too.

You can see the power of the concept, and of clearing away anything that might be stopping you from pursuing higher income and higher impact activity.

Almost as a natural progression, if you can identify who your ideal clients are, identify what it is they want and then innovate your business to give those ideal clients what they want, you will slowly but surely begin to replace the remaining 80% of your not-so-ideal clients with those who will spend the most money with you, stay with you forever and in the process, increase your revenue and profits without adding any major time or effort.

Perhaps the most intriguing and enjoyable part of the Pareto Principle is that to get vastly better results, you do not have to do anything differently except perhaps shift your focus. You just have to do more of the particular elements you are already doing fantastically well. The end result will be that you work less and earn more.

Which takes us back to the beginning and the vital importance of psychographics. Those psychographics help you to understand why those 20% of your ideal clients buy from you and when you have that understanding, you can follow the steps in this chapter to start attracting more of them with compelling marketing.

7. Persuasion Marketing

Persuasion marketing is about presenting compelling information and offers about your product or service that will persuade prospects to take a specific action. It should be part of your sales process.

With persuasion marketing, the key is to address the desires of your ideal clients in such a way that you continue to add value based on the benefits that they want and along the way, you create a sales process that will continue to move them through the various stages of the decision-making process.

As we discussed, most messages are not compelling and they focus on the features of the product or service, rather than the benefits to the ideal clients. They work by appealing to logic, whereas your message should focus on the benefits to your ideal clients and as a result, should be emotions-based.

We covered much of this when we looked at crafting an elevator pitch and a USP. Within this segment on persuasion marketing, we will go past the process of interrupting your prospects with a compelling hot button message and engaging them with a suggested solution and benefits. What comes next in persuading prospects into your final distribution channels are the processes of educating and then offering.

Great marketing is an art. Look at Apple and what they have done to market computers and phones that were previously utilitarian, transforming them into items that are pleasurable and intuitive to use. But luckily, there is also an element of science to marketing.

The Marketing Equation:

Interrupt + Engage + Educate + Offer = Success

Your marketing messages need to:

Interrupt your prospects from what they are doing by touching on their deepest concerns and issues with a striking message that relates specifically to them.

Engage your prospects by giving them an immediate sense that the solution you are offering is the one they are looking for.

Educate your prospects about your products and services and especially about how your offering is unique and extraordinary.

Offer something of value to them that gives them no risk and that proves to them that what you can do is real and has integrity.

As we discussed, your marketing messages are not aiming at anyone and everyone. They should only resonate with your ideal client. An emotionally-targeted hot button message encourages qualified prospects to learn more.

There are ways to set up your marketing materials, from flyers to brochures to adverts, that make use of these four steps using headlines, sub headlines, some benefit-driven main copy and an unbeatable offer.

Our builder might easily make up flyers to drop into homes in the neighborhood he serves, using his USP as the basis for a compelling headline, and a variation on his longer elevator pitch as the sub headline and copy. The site we run at EBS Digital University (www.ebsdigitaluniversity.com) has a number of templates for various business categories, ready to use. It is a stand alone membership program, but we offer it to our EBS Digital customers for free to provide businesses with the tools to create their own sales process and to help them move quickly through all the stages I've gone over here - and as a result their online marketing conversions from traffic to sales inevitably increase dramatically.

I have gone into more detail about applying the marketing equation in the following section which deals with online marketing, and more specifically I've looked at it in the context of how to construct a great landing page for your website.

In the meantime, let me move the focus here away from the marketing message and back to the innovations you need to put into your business. In the end, if you can offer genuinely exceptional value and a creative innovation or two in your business, you will never struggle to create compelling marketing.

Nothing keeps clients with your business more effectively than offering them more value than they pay for in the cash price. Doing this in a way that makes financial sense to your business is one of the main things you will have looked at while innovating your business.

So I would like to end this section on Persuasion Marketing by offering a few more ideas for you as to how to to innovate your business, because that is the core from which your persuasiveness grows - and if you have genuine value and difference, people sense it and find it persuasive.

So here are several areas you can think about and apply to your specific business and market - use them as stimulation for your creativity and brainstorm as much as you can:

Can You Save Time?

Most people value time today more than money. How available are you to your prospects? How can you make working with you easier for their schedules?

Can You Streamline Your Order Process?

Amazon and others have set quite a standard. However, technology and customer relationship software makes many of the systems you need available on a small budget. At the end of the day, ordering from your website should be easy. And if ordering, whether online, by phone or in person, is not easy in your industry generally, making it simple can help you be a leader in your market.

Could You Deliver Your Service or Product Differently?

Perhaps you could set up a convenient location? Or find a way to deliver products that are normally collected, thereby tapping into the all important time-saving benefits for prospects at the same time.

You could also consider electronic delivery for certain items or create new products that can be delivered via your website or by email.

Also in this category, think about whether you can offer a more secure or safe payment or delivery method than is standard in your industry. In a world of internet security concerns, reliable payments mean a lot to prospects.

Can You Offer Payment Terms?

Especially if other companies in your category don't offer terms, you can differentiate your business by offering payment terms over 30, 60 or 90 days. Or by spreading payments over a few weeks or months.

Can You Offer a Related Service?

With EBS Digital, we started out offering mainly SEO and online marketing. Soon we found that clients wanted to change their sites to build landing pages or add online stores to take advantage of the new traffic they gained. So we added a development team and a group of dynamic designers so we could offer a full web service that was integrated and worked well together.

Can You Offer Some Education or Assistance?

Prospects place great value on learning skills, methods or ideas that will make a difference to their lives. If you know a way to help people benefit longer term, share it with them as a book, a course, a report or a podcast.

Can You Offer Extras?

What would be a relatively small, related extra you could add that would leave your clients feeling looked after, and that you could make prospects aware of? What if our builder trained his workers to spend 10 minutes at the end of each day cleaning up the dust they'd created and making the house feel livable again?

Can You Remove the Risk?

If someone can buy from you and feel no sense of risk at all, they are more likely to convert from a prospect to a customer. Try to offer something that is better than most others in your field. Like our builder who offers money back for running over time. Or a money back guarantee for a product.

Any of these innovations will be a great start to building your persuasive marketing messages. We'll look more at how to do that and how to distribute those messages online in the following section.

You started your business to have the freedom to enjoy the lifestyle that you want. Most entrepreneurs are busy working in their business instead of on their business and they are just too busy to take time out to evaluate the business or to put systems and processes in place. It's understandable, but by setting aside even an hour or two a week to step out of the mayhem and into a state where you can really think about the direction and the core of your marketing, you will be able to make exponential strides that will surprise you with their power. Having a clear sales process will help you take your business to new heights and will help make your goals into a reality.

Section 2
INTERNET MARKETING

To grow your business and to grow your profit in today's economy, you need to have a detailed and defined online marketing strategy.

The number of people on the internet is growing. In the developing world, mobile phones have become the dominant method of access to the internet, and everywhere the number of people using the internet to find local businesses is growing exponentially. A Google search is now mobile and available everywhere. It is free and usually very accurate.

97 percent of Americans who use the internet, use it to shop or at least, to gather information before making a shopping decision. Most of us go online to get more details about a product or a service that we are interested in, to check the features and benefits it provides, compare prices, selection and warranties - and only then do we begin to think seriously about making the actual purchase.

There is something at play here that is far more important than the sheer volume of people using the internet to make decisions and choices.

What is truly revolutionary is the **way** people now make decisions. Where business owners used to be far more in control of how people consumed their adverts and content, now decisions are driven much more by the consumer. Good advertising can take you so far, but the word of mouth approvals and reviews on social media sites count too. 78% of Facebook users trust the recommendations of people they are connected to. Only 14% trust the ads on Facebook. That does not mean you should dismiss the power of social media ads, which is still a substantial power, but it does show that an authentic appreciation of your products and services can be an enormous benefit to you when you use social media.

Marketing on the internet is not an option anymore. It is a necessity. If you are without an online presence, or not doing very much with your website, you are missing out on a very deep and targeted pool of potential customers.

Unfortunately, out of the 30 million small businesses in

the United States, over 90 percent of them have no online marketing strategy whatsoever. The online revolution has happened very quickly, and with incredible speed, so not having a strategy is nothing to feel bad about, but you do need to address it.

The biggest hurdle many small business owners face is that internet marketing is one of a hundred other things you need to handle, and often you have no clear idea exactly where to begin.

Some business owners might fear change, and worry about how to stay on top of online changes which happen daily. The internet is a massive web of content, media and social networking; it can be intimidating or daunting at best to try to imagine how to get your business seen amongst it all.

So why should you bother? Because, on the plus side, technology has leveled the playing field in many ways.

In the past, most small businesses lacked the resources of their larger competitors. Today, however, even a small business can access much of the same technology as the giant corporations. They can utilize the internet and social media on the same terms as anyone else; they can tap into the potential of email marketing, cater to the wants of their customers by accepting online payments and sometimes even deliver products, information and gifts over the Internet electronically, reducing the cost of production and distribution.

Dealing with all these aspects of online marketing is actually a wonderful opportunity, especially when you have been used to dealing with offline advertising media such as newspapers, magazines, radio and TV. These have their place, but they simply do not offer the same potential for targeting your ideal consumer as online marketing does, leaving a large percentage of your marketing dollars wasted with a 'spray and pray' approach.

We talked about identifying your ideal customers in the previous section. The key to excelling with online marketing is to ensure you target exactly those customers.

When you work with Search Engine Optimization or Pay Per Click ads, you target those customers by defining your key terms and phrases based on your ideal client profile and you use them as the basis for your site content, your marketing focus, your ads and optimization work. This is an enormous advantage, and it is one of the reasons I have placed such an emphasis on taking the time to know your ideal client before you start your online or offline marketing. Your conversions and results simply go through the roof.

Online marketing is not a magic bullet. But it is an essential part of your sales and marketing and once you have taken a little time to think through the process, the potential for growth is incredible.

There are many benefits to marketing your business online and let's take a quick overview of the advantages:

1. The internet lets you define your niche market and cater to it

The internet has opened up all sorts of niche marketing opportunities that never existed before, or were previously too expensive for small businesses to use. Defining that niche is not difficult, as we've seen in the previous section, but it takes some time and thought on your part and it is one of the first processes we encourage our clients to undertake when they begin search engine optimization with us, because it gives you the benefit of increased site traffic made up of prospects who are genuinely keen to use your product or service.

2. Your website can create an excellent first impression for your business

With a professionally designed website, a small business on the Internet can feel as knowledgeable and credible, or even more so, than a large corporation. In fact, when you understand the basic principles of persuasion marketing, a small business using these principles can attract the same customers as larger corporations.

If a purchase is of a higher value item, or something associated with the need for specialization (like a lawyer or doctor), ensuring that your company comes across in a way that is reassuring to your prospect is extremely important.

During this section, you will find out how to structure your landing and home pages so that prospects can obtain immediate value from you without any risk to them. This strategy allows you to have a website that makes an excellent first impression and also one that generates leads and sales.

3. The cost of advertising is lower

Compared to other forms of more traditional media, the internet enables a business to advertise at considerably lower prices. Pay per click ads on the major search engines are generally much less expensive than advertising on television, radio, or in newspapers, magazines and even direct mail. More importantly, you will be targeting customers who use search terms for their requirements that your business can meet and so your online advertising is extremely finely targeted.

4. Maintaining a good relationship with your existing customers is cost effective

Sending out a physical mailing to your customers can cost from $1.50 each and much more when you take into account printing, postage, handling and so on. The same message sent by email costs nothing. The format of the email, the content and the approach can all help you to nurture your customers and remind them that you are concerned about their requirements.

I should say here that handwritten notes are still wonderful to receive, even more so now that we are used to sending everything, even thank you notes and holiday cards, by email. So they have a place too in making clients feel very appreciated. But as a day-to-day tool, email is effective and inexpensive.

5. You can create leads and income while you sleep

Another benefit of online marketing and maintaining your online presence involves the fact that you can do business 24/7. Small business owners must and can begin to think on a global level. Unless you offer very local services, if you are a doctor or an osteopath for instance, many businesses can sell their products and services to a more widespread audience.

Even a localized business can look at producing a book or CD or even a DVD which can deliver the benefit of their experience and expertise to a worldwide audience and that can sell from their site (and from bigger sites like Amazon or ebay) all day and night.

By automating your website, your business can operate 24 hours a day, 7 days a week, and often with no additional staff costs. Your prospects are online looking for solutions, products and services every minute of the day. Placing your business online gives you the ability to position your company in front of this global audience of prospects.

Automating your site can be as simple as ensuring that you have web forms to capture a prospect's request for information or quotes, or installing a system which can automate months of email contact, keeping your business supplying prospects with a flow of helpful content that keeps you uppermost in their minds when they are ready to buy.

YOUR ROADMAP FOR ONLINE MARKETING

So let's navigate through what to do and how to do it in a set of clear stages.

STEP 1: Design and deploy a content-driven, interactive website. If you already have a site, then this stage can be about re-evaluating how your site can work harder for your business to capture interest and inspire prospects to contact you before they leave your site.

STEP 2: Build an integrated campaign to bring more inbound traffic to your site, based on one or more core strategies such as organic Search Engine Optimization, and Pay Per Click ads.

STEP 3: Utilize the intimacy and reach of Social Media to build lasting relationships with your prospects and clients.

STEP 4: Measure everything; be willing to adapt and evolve. If a tactic does not work, either make changes or try a different course of action altogether.

This section will look at the first 2 steps in detail and we will look at social media, Step 3, in the next chapter.

Step 1: Building A Website That Works

How many times have you been drawn into a site that attracted you, without even being able to articulate why? Conversely, how often have you immediately navigated away from a site that gave you a bad feeling, or was too cluttered for you to find what you wanted immediately?

Your website is the cornerstone for all your marketing activities, the place where you begin to convert ideal prospects into ideal customers. Your website should:

1. Establish your business's credibility.

2. Let visitors know straightaway what content they can find and what they can do on the site. The main website navigation should be clear and easy to understand, while features such as the newsletter sign-up should be positioned where visitors typically expect them to be (top right sidebar).

3. Lastly, your website should connect visitors to your social media channels and provide ways for them to interact with you - as well as with each other. The site should work for search engines (no broken links, slow loading or duplicate content) and be accessible to anyone using any device (desktop computer, mobile, Ipad) or any browser (Internet Explorer, Firefox, Chrome, Safari).

15 Steps to a Great Website:

1. Select a unique domain name

A .com address is the most common domain and the one most associated with companies who are leaders in their niche markets.

But many successful online brands have used non-traditional domains to make themselves memorable (for example, the music service Last.fm) so there is plenty of room for creativity.

Most hosting providers offer domains for free along with their monthly or annual packages. Alternatively, you can purchase your domain inexpensively through a service like MyDomain or Dynadot. Protect your brand by buying as many domain variations as you can afford.

The best domain names are short and easy to remember and the most ideal ones for search optimization could also have an indication of your business's product or service in the title. For instance 'smithandcompany.com' is fine, but 'smithroofbuilders.com' can be more helpful because it contains a keyword.

Names of domains can also give a sense of your company culture so consider that too. 'Smithandcompany' might give a slightly more formal, established air than 'Smithandco' or even 'thesmithbiz' where you would expect a young, playful or tech company. These are not hard and fast rules but since a large number of names may be available for you to choose from, it is a smaller note to keep in mind.

If you have an existing domain name for your business you can change or update it. There is some benefit to choosing a domain name that has keywords in it, but if you have been around for a long time your customers and prospects may not react well to a change. Additionally, the length of time your website has been online will have a bearing on your search engine rankings. If you do update your domain, you can redirect your old website to your new one using a 301 redirect which a developer can do for you.

2. Choose a hosting service

There are lots of good, affordable website hosting plans available. Do some research before you decide. You want a service that is fast, secure and has excellent server "uptime".

As video becomes more popular and useful for searches, more businesses are making and hosting their own videos on their sites. You may want to consider a cloud hosting plan to protect you against slow service or crashes from traffic spikes. An even easier alternative is to embed videos on your site from your YouTube or Vimeo account, or to use a service like Easy Video Player, which hosts the videos for you and lets you add marketing tools like sign up forms directly into your video.

3. Select a CMS platform

Before you design and build your website, select a CMS platform. Content Management Systems (CMS) have revolutionized web development, because they allow anyone to create, publish, and manage content online. The three major content management systems are Drupal, Joomla and WordPress. Most web designers or developers have a preference for one or the other. Make sure that you are comfortable with their recommendation by testing the platform ahead of time. If you are planning to do most of your updates yourself, then WordPress is currently one of the most user-friendly formats.

4. Choose a theme or template

With the proliferation of ready-made themes and templates, you do not have to hire a designer for your website. But as soon as you stray outside the template offerings, it can be more time consuming to produce your site. If you are using WordPress as your CMS, there are a large number of free and premium themes to style your website.

Alternatively, use this stage to research sites that you like the look of and to decide why and what you like about them. Visual cues help vastly reduce the time a good designer takes to interpret your desires.

5. Hire a designer/developer

You may still want to hire a designer/developer to customize your website for that fully "branded" feel. I am a big advocate of using a good designer because what they can bring to the table in terms of giving your business a look that keeps your visitors on the site can be invaluable.

Take a look at the designer's portfolio and make sure they know how to develop the kinds of forms, e-stores or other items that you want for your site. Also try to have them send their standard questionnaire to you as it will give you an idea of how they will interact and collect ideas and content from you. You want efficiency as well as design talent, and I have seen many companies languish for months designing and developing a site that could have taken a few weeks at most.

6. Design your site for people

This sounds obvious, but usability is both an art and science. What is good usability?

- A clear and simple navigation system
- Clear links and calls to action
- Easily scannable content

7. Decide on a navigation style and layout

You do not want people who come to your site to even think for a moment about where they can go and how to get there. If visitors cannot immediately find what they are looking for, they will leave, often within seconds. For your site navigation:

- Keep the structure of your primary navigation simple, clean and at the top of your page, or possibly on the left hand side.
- Include full navigation to all pages in the footer of your site.
- Use breadcrumb navigation on each page so your visitors are aware of their navigation trail.
- Don't offer too many navigation options on a single page.
- Keep your navigation three levels deep at the most.
- Steer away from complex JavaScript or Flash for your navigation. Many mobile phones cannot see Flash (yet) and some browsers might need a Flash update.

8. Design a consistent layout

Ensure that your important links, images and text are 'above the fold'. Of course, now that we all use the internet on different sized devices, 'the fold' is not a clear concept to define, but the idea is to get the major content and your call to action in the top section of your page.

The main elements on your site should be consistent across all pages including colors, sizes, layout and placement of text and images. Colors and fonts should be primarily the same and navigation should remain in the same location throughout your website.

There are typically three variations of page layouts for most websites: one for the homepage, one for content pages and one for form pages. If you can keep the elements in these layouts constant, it will help to keep your visitors from feeling lost.

9. Add a blog

Blogging is one of the most important assets for inbound marketing to your website. There are a number of reasons for this:

- Blogs create fresh content and more content, both of which are helpful for SEO.
- They help to establish you as an authority in your market.
- They are an excellent way to engage with your audience and customers.
- They can be a very good source of valuable inbound links. If other sites like your content, they will link to it, and that link back to your site is very helpful for search engine rankings.
- They help drive more traffic and leads back to your website.

With reference to that last point, just take a moment to look at these figures from Hubspot:

- B2C businesses that blog generate 88% more leads per month than businesses that do not blog.
- Companies that blog typically have 55% more site visitors than companies that do not have a blog.

I hope that convinces you to start a blog or be more regular with the blog you currently have. CMS systems like WordPress have a blog as a built-in feature. If you have a static site, you can use WordPress to add a blog feature.

If you host your blog on an external site like wordpress.com or blogger.com, that is fine but you will miss some of the added benefits of increased traffic and enhanced SEO for your main website.

10. Burn your RSS feed with Feedburner

Once your website is built, burn your RSS (Real Simple Syndication) feed with FeedBurner. To create a FeedBurner account, you will need to have a Google account. Manually add a redirect from your original feed to your new FeedBurner feed, or install the FeedBurner FeedSmith plugin to do this automatically.

If that sounds like work it is worth it. FeedBurner lets visitors sign-up to receive your news feed by email. This is important as many people are still unfamiliar with what is involved in subscribing to an RSS feed. FeedBurner also tells you how many people are subscribed to your feed. It automatically "pings" the search engines to let them know when new content has been added.

11. Add an email subscription box

Encourage email subscriptions on your website by adding an opt-in email subscription box. The upper-right corner of the page is usually a good spot and it should appear on all the main pages of your website, including your blog. When creating your email subscription box, ask only for the information you absolutely need (i.e. an email address) as this will vastly increase the number of people willing to sign up.

12. Enable social sharing

Social media websites have seen exponential growth and continue to grow larger every day. Allowing people to "Like" a post, product, or blog entry, causes a user's friends to see what they like and even gives them a link to find it themselves.

The Facebook "Like" box widget can be customized and added to your site's sidebar. The embed code can be found from Facebook Share. The "Like" box allows you to acquire new fans for your Facebook page without them having to leave your website.

Making it easy for people to share your content and resources will increase your flow of traffic and even more so if your content is top quality.

You can easily add a sharing widget on every page on your site that will let visitors share your pages via all the major social networks. Tools like AddThis or ShareThis are easy to install and provide you with analytic tracking as well.

13. Add your Twitter stream

Another way to extend the reach of your website is to add a Twitter badge. The Twitter badge shows your real-time Twitter stream and provides a link to your Twitter account. We will look at how to make good use of Twitter, and other social media platforms, a little later in this section.

14. Add a row of social media icons

Add a row of social media icons to your sidebar and then link the images to your most important social media channels (Facebook, Flickr, Twitter, YouTube, etc.). Make sure that your buttons are "above the fold" and large enough to be visible. There are numerous plugins that let you add and customize this feature. It is always good to include your RSS feed in your "social" row.

15. Make your site mobile friendly

This is essential as more of us get accustomed to being online everywhere and anywhere. There are several plugins available (for WordPress) to help "mobilize" your site, including the WordPress Mobile Pack, Mobify, Mofuse and WPTouch.

You can use the above as a check list to ensure that you incorporate all the necessary elements. But there is a lot more to consider about how you use the site and what content you choose to make it work most effectively for your business.

How To Make Sure Your Site Creates Leads and Makes Money

So once you have a website that incorporates most or all of the above elements, how do you then turn that site into an inbound marketing tool? A website needs not just to exist, but to perform. It needs to attract visitors, educate them and convince them to buy.

Today, the web is social and extremely interactive and convenient for users. Buyers want information when they want it and how they want it and usually without the involvement of a sales person. They want to learn more and not experience a hard sell.

Results show that inbound marketing has a 62% less cost per lead compared to outbound, or traditional, marketing. That is a very significant difference to your bottom line.

How important is your website in all of this? Usually, your site acts as a single unifying place where traffic from blogs, social media, SEO and PPC ads converge.

So how do you organize your site content to make a difference to your marketing? Again, it is always good to have the end in mind, so when you are putting together the content, try asking yourself:

- Will people know what I do within seconds?
- Will they understand what page they are on and what it's about?
- Will they know what to do next?
- Why should they buy/subscribe/download from this site instead of from someone else?

If you can answer all these, you will be in good shape because ideally, you want visitors to know what your site is about, what they can do there and why they should take action.

Practical Steps to Creating Content That Engages

1. Create a few headline and sub-headline ideas for your most important pages. Use a powerful value proposition based on the benefits that you provide to the niche market we defined in the last section, and try to steer clear of cliches. Your USP might work well as a headline, or an abbreviation of your elevator pitch.

2. Make sure to include clear calls-to-action and logical next steps. Include links in your body copy, links at the end of the copy and calls-to-action wherever appropriate.

3. Educate and Offer Value. Even though the purpose of your website might be to provide information about your products and services, not everyone is ready to buy when they first come to your site. And more and more, users expect to be able to receive some benefits before they buy.

4. Offer Extra Content. As part of offering some benefit up front, extra content that you can offer could include eBooks, white papers, videos, and other forms of content that are educational. This nurtures prospects through your marketing and sales funnel until they are ready to buy and it shows goodwill to prospects when you offer them genuinely valuable information without requiring a sale. If you don't know where to start, consider writing an 8 or 10 point one pager that gives people specialized information about the issues they might be facing.

5. Write as if you are speaking directly to your audience. The more you can reflect your own character and personality the more people will feel trust and engagement. On a practical level, using words like 'I' and 'We' is a good start. Just as we all like to have conversations with people who show an interest in us, your content should be more focused on your visitors and what they are looking for rather than the features you provide. Also, the power of

storytelling cannot be overestimated to connect you with your audience. Describe how you understand what they feel now and explain how you found the solution and what it meant to you.

6. The quality of content must be high. Your content should provide some value or educational meaning that is helpful to site visitors. It should be as unique as possible, and fresh. You can usually tell when a site still has content from two years ago and it doesn't usually leave you with a good feeling.

7. Do use FAQs. It is good customer service, because nine times out of ten, the unanswered questions or objections or uncertainties that your customer has can be answered with an FAQ page and it saves them having to contact you and wait for a response. Think about the questions customers tend to ask you often, or put yourself in their shoes and think about any worries they might have about your product or service if they did not know you well, and they had never used you before.

8. Be clear, always. As consumers we are sophisticated and unlikely to find advertising cliches and surreptitious or aggressive persuasion appealing. If you focus your content on being clear, more people will place their trust in you. Try not to make things more complicated than they need to be. Your goal is to be understood. Just be upfront with what you want people to do on your site. If you want them to buy from you, give them some irresistible and true reasons why you feel you do a better job than anyone else. You will gain more fans and followers in the long term.

Your Site and Persuasion Marketing

Your prospects are not all at the same stage in their decision-making process.

Some are ready to make an immediate decision (typically no more than 4%) while others (96%) are still doing their research on you. And you have no way of knowing where they are in their decision-making process.

Those who are not quite ready to engage or to buy immediately need nurturing.

Persuasion Marketing addresses all their wants and needs and continues to move them through the various stages of their decision-making process.

If that sounds vague, it can be crystallized into the more scientific equation that we first looked at in the previous section; because marketing is an art, but it is also a science:

The Marketing Equation;

Interrupt + Engage + Educate + Offer

We went over these steps in Section 1, but now let's apply the equation in the context of constructing a website landing page. The marketing messages on your site landing pages should:

Interrupt:

The primary purpose here is to grab the prospect's attention, so that the rest of your message will be received.

A great headline that addresses your prospect's hot buttons is an obvious way to 'interrupt' on a home page or landing page.

It addresses a major problem, fear or frustration that your prospects generally experience just before they buy what you sell.

When written correctly, the right headline has a second function that many marketers and business owners do not think about; it immediately **qualifies** your ideal client and **disqualifies** those prospects who are not ideal clients, which saves you marketing time and money. You have fewer people who move to engage with you, but those that do are much more likely to cross over and work with you.

Engage:

This is where a good **sub-headline** can take your message a step further and provide important, decision-making information. It should build on the impact of the headline and make the visitor want to read further.

Here is an example of interrupting and engaging with a headline and sub headline:

'Would You Like a Builder Who Is On Time, On Budget and Guarantees His Work?'

'We pay you for every day we run over schedule and if anything goes wrong, we'll come back and fix it for free'

It certainly is likely to compel people to read to the next part of the page.

Educate:

Next you need to demonstrate how your business delivers on the promises you just made in the headline and sub-headline

This main content is the lengthiest text in your marketing. But do remember that the body copy details your case by presenting evidence. You cannot just claim that you give the best value, you have to prove it.

And by now, we know not to make too much of the features that you offer. Those are important but try to present them from the perspective of the benefit to the consumer. Instead of saying that you always finish a building job on time, you can explain that you pay your clients $100 for every day you run over schedule.

Another example might be if you ran a private school. You might say that you have the best teachers to provide an excellent education. Or you could say that 80% of your graduating students get the highest grade on their final exams and that 95% of them attend the university or college of their first choice. These are two very different ways of saying the same thing, and the latter paints a clearer picture in the minds of concerned parents.

This kind of content could be based on the long elevator pitch that we created in the previous section.

Every prospect is always looking for the best value. That is not the lowest price but the most value for the price.

Offer:

Provide one specific, low risk, easy to take, call to action (CTA) that helps visitors make a good decision. Having a free report to download, or an offer that has exceptional value will help people to start a relationship with your business.

CTAs are usually high up on a page so that visitors know where to take the next step without scrolling down. Here are a few guidelines on making a CTA work on your site:

- Make them bigger and bolder than most other elements on the page, but don't overdo it.
- Consider the colors of the CTA link or button and how they work with the rest of your site. It may seem obvious to say, but if they look good, bold but not overly aggressive, people will want to click on them.
- Offer CTAs that provide value, like guides, white papers, estimates."Contact Us" is a poor CTA and

it is better not to rely on it as your only option for conversion.

- Make the CTA look as if it can be clicked. You can do this by making a button or adding a hover effect to an element. Remember that certain colors can work in your favor (green has the connotation 'go' for many people, while a red circle usually signifies 'stop' in most cultures).
- Test whenever you can. Try testing different colors, language and placement to see which CTAs get more clicks and drive more leads.

It is also important to keep in mind that you have to make an offer that feels right. Asking visitors to buy a high priced item as soon as they arrive at your site is unlikely to work. In that situation, offering more information or a guide or a free report would be reassuring.

Whatever you offer should be available upon request and it should require the visitor to input their email details, so there is an exchange - you offer information of value in exchange for an email address that you can continue to market to.

The more value you offer, the more information you can request. Many visitors do not like to part with their phone numbers for a free report. But if you are shipping a physical book for instance, that value suggests that you can request an address and phone number if only to ensure it reaches your prospects.

Websites Versus Landing Pages

Your website's home page is the first page your prospects come to. It tells them who you are and what your business is all about.

A typical website home page offers many options and an arriving prospect is often bombarded with information, links, offers and images.

Even if you have a very clean design, your home page

usually contains a fair amount of information.

By contrast, **a landing page has one sole purpose which is to capture leads**. This is why landing pages are created especially for use in specific marketing campaigns.

For instance, you might target a key phrase like 'free building report' through SEO. If you drive a user to your more generic home page when they click on that keyword, where the report sign up is not immediately obvious alongside all the text or information on offer, they could leave or 'bounce' from your site very quickly.

If you set up a separate landing page where the sign up box for the free report is center stage, visitors will feel reassured in their expectations and that keeps them with you. Conversion rates from pay-per-click are increased by as much as 50% with well-designed landing pages and yet less than 20% of all sites use them.

You'll see why this is even more important for PPC, where your ad must link to specific landing pages to reinforce the message and your offer contained in the ad.

You basically want to make sure your prospects know that they have come to the right place and to save your prospects time and effort, both of which are appreciated by internet users everywhere.

Landing Page Basics:

1. A headline and (optional) sub-headline
2. A brief description of the offer/CTA
3. At least one supporting image
4. Optional extra elements such as testimonials or security badges
5. And most importantly, a form to capture information

Make Your Landing Page Effective:

- Include the elements above and only those. Keep your pages simple and minimize distractions.

- Do not use your homepage as a landing page.

- Remove the main site navigation from the landing page so that your visitors can focus on completing the form rather than exploring your site. Just keep your company logo as a signal that they are on your site. Google dislikes pages with no navigation for search, but that might not be a major concern if you are driving people to a landing page from a link or a PPC campaign. A good compromise strategy might be to place your links in the footer rather than the header of the page.

- Make it very clear what the offer is and make it irresistible and benefit driven to your prospects.

- Absolutely make sure that the content on your landing page matches your call to action. If there is a disconnect in your messaging, you will lose visitors.

- Only collect the information you absolutely need.

Landing Page Offers:

Forms are the key to a landing page and they give a clear signal to the visitor about what they are being asked to do.

The fewer fields you have in a form, the more likely you are to convert visitors to sign ups because a longer form looks like more work and sometimes people avoid it all together. The advantage of having a carefully chosen extra field or two is that it can help qualify or filter your leads further.

- The more valuable an offer is (and if you communicate the value well), the more information you can usually ask for in return. A newsletter subscription generally should only ask for an email address and possibly a first name.

- Examples of CTA offers for a landing page are asking people to register for an event, complete an information request form, download a white paper or report, subscribe to an online newsletter, get a free informational video or request a sales call.

- Reduce concerns with a privacy message (or a link to your privacy policy) that indicates that their email will not be shared or sold.

- Avoid writing "SUBMIT" on your form buttons. It does not have a proactive connotation even if people have become used to it. Try "Download Report," "Get your free eBook," or "Join our newsletter."

- If your CTA offers a download of some kind, fulfill the request instantly with a link to the download on the next page. You can send an automatic email with a link to the offer but offers sometimes get lost in the junk folder, and it adds another layer for people to cross to access your material.

Once you have started to build your list of leads and newsletter sign ups, you should make a plan to keep in touch with them.

Set a date monthly, or twice monthly, to send them additional and compelling information that adds something to their knowledge base.

These drip campaigns are now more usually called 'lead nurture campaigns' and that change in terminology should reflect in your content and approach. Your emails should not be attempting to sell, only to educate about your innovations and the benefits they provide.

You can send these emails more frequently, but there is a danger that people will not read them, even if they perceive the value, because they come to their inbox too often, and they rely on receiving the next one a few days later.

STEP 2: Build an integrated campaign to bring more inbound traffic to your site

Strategies to Flow More Traffic to Your Site:

The major ways in which traffic can be sent to your website are:

1. Search Engine referrals through natural results - where people click through to your site after finding that you rank high for certain search terms on Google, Bing or Yahoo. This accounts for the vast majority of site visits.

2. Referrals from other sites - if your website has a link from another site, that link can be used by interested prospects to click through to your site. This method is dependent on other sites linking to yours, and it is tied to the traffic and feel of those sites.

3. Referrals from Social Media sites - this is a growing source of traffic. YouTube is second only to Google in the volume of searches it carries, and prospects who find your business on Facebook, LinkedIn or Twitter can click to your site - so always make sure your URL is displayed and linked.

4. Pay Per Click or similar online ads - you pay within an agreed budget and based on your resulting rankings and the competition for the search terms you select, you pay each time someone clicks on your ad and through to your site.

Surprisingly though, the majority of companies that build a new site give very little thought to how their prospects will find them online. Having a site is a good start but it needs traffic to complete its purpose, so let's look now at the most efficient ways to get that traffic.

Search Engine Optimization (SEO)

The strongest source of traffic for most businesses is through natural rankings on search engines. Of all the search engines available online, Google, Yahoo! and Bing are the three that dominate in terms of traffic. While data varies by country, these three account for about 95% of all searches done online.

When searching for information:

- more than 40% of users click on the number 1 spot in the search engine results.

- 1.5% of users click on the number 10 spot on the search.

- Less than 1% click on pages 2 and 3 and beyond.

How does that make a difference to your business?

If you rank number one for a keyword that generates 2000 searches per month, **that could be the difference between 25 people finding your site or 800 people finding it.**

If you currently convert 1 in every 25 site visitors to become a client, that could add up to 32 new clients per month instead of just 1.

If the lifetime value of one of your customers is $1000, that's an increase in revenue of over $30,000 from one month at number 1 for 1 keyword.

What would that do for your cash flow?

When harnessed correctly, with a targeted approach, that is the power of good, ethical SEO.

Driving traffic - qualified, meaningful, traffic - to your site has a number of major benefits:

1. It boosts your profile within your industry.

2. It establishes your business as an authority in your niche market.

3. It makes a much larger pool of your ideal prospects aware of your products and services.

But getting more traffic to your site is only one side of the equation. Converting those visitors to leads and sales is, of course, key. While most companies are accustomed to viewing their online marketing budget as a cost, you should aim to convert that cost into an investment - one that will increase your income, your cash flow and your freedom.

With SEO, we run a three step process at EBS Digital, all of which I will detail in this chapter so that you can do it alone, or ask your current company if they are following all of these strategies. Our aim is for our clients to:

- Dominate the rankings for your chosen keywords
- Dominate your niche market
- Drastically increase your revenue

Step 3 is all about conversion and we encourage our clients at EBS Digital to focus on this by giving them free access to hundreds of resources and a customized roadmap on a members-only site that works on their messaging, identifying their ideal client and the entire process we outlined in section 2 of this book. It is the part most online marketing companies ignore.

Good SEO takes time to get results - from 4 to 6 months in general, though sometimes results start to show faster. SEO should be part of your ongoing online marketing process and it should not start and then stop when rankings are achieved as those rankings will go down again if not maintained.

It takes a fair amount of time and technical ability as well. Some companies try to take shortcuts to minimize the cost or quality of their labour, but it rarely works. The term 'black hat' is used for optimization techniques which contradict Google's rules and suggestions by using faster but less ethical and ultimately less successful methods of trying to boost rankings. Often, such techniques will get your site blocked by Google entirely, and getting it ranked again is a very long and painful process.

Search engines are perceived to be relatively unbiased. They have a specific set of criteria that they use to rank pages, which we will look at here, but one business cannot out-rank the other by paying Google. Google's reputation and entire business rests on delivering the most relevant websites for users' search queries.

In order to make sure they secure loyal traffic from internet searchers, their programmers are continuously trying to find ways to provide the most relevant, accurate listings in response to search queries.

So how can search engines comb through all of the content on the Internet, decide what is important, and categorize it according to what people type into the search field? It is a complex algorithm and a complex process.

Search engines use little spiders (also known as robots or crawlers) - small software programs that sift through the Internet to index pages and find relevant websites.

Search engine spiders are constantly being upgraded to improve their ability to deliver relevant search results. Each search engine has its own proprietary algorithm that is highly valuable and that is never shared or distributed.

Search engines display query listings in order of relevance, as determined by their spiders or crawlers. The primary ways they determine relevance are:

1. Authority: If the site is an authority on a particular subject, then other sites on the same subject will link to it. These links act like "votes," with some links being worth more votes than others.

2 . Main Focus/Relevance: Is the subject the primary or secondary focus of the site? For example, a builder with a sub-page that sells building supplies would have a primary focus on building services and secondary focus on selling supplies. This is determined through the structure of the site and the concepts on the main pages versus the sub-pages.

3. Content: How many pages are about the particular subject or topic? Which pages are they? Are they linked from the home page, or buried deeper in the site?

4. Relative Score: All of this data is collected and ranked next to other pages. The site that is more relevant, based on this score, will appear higher in the rankings.

5. Age: How long has the website been live?

6. Quality: How valuable is the content? Is it frequently updated? Is there plenty of content?

Knowing many of the details and logistics of SEO as I now do, I have learned that it is a specialist job.

I have to admit that I have never sat down and rewritten my own site code, or renamed my header or alt tags or interlinked content.

I am in no way a techie, and my logic for having someone else do the technical part of SEO for me, is that it gives me more time doing what I do best - marketing the visible part of the site.

I look at it the same way as I look at my contracts or tax returns. As business owners we keep an eye on these but we rarely draw up our own complicated legal work or do our own taxes. Tax laws change every year and the level of detail required to produce a strong contract, or to minimize your tax payment is high. You tend to go to a trusted lawyer or accountant for that - to specialists - so that you can have time to do what you do best - work on your business.

It is much the same with online marketing, which is a world that moves very fast. To keep up with it can be fun but it is also challenging, and it helps to have access to a team who spend their time concerned with the minute changes that Google decides to place on their algorithms, so that you have time to grow your business and perhaps focus on the more personalized aspects of online marketing, like updating social media profiles and so on.

But if you are excited about getting to grips with your own online marketing and are a hands on kind of person, I will outline in this next chapter the basic work flow that you need to follow when doing SEO, so you can find out exactly what is involved and implement the same tasks yourself if you have the time and would like to.

1. Keyword Analysis

Choosing your keywords is arguably the most important part of SEO (and also Pay Per Click ads)

Deciding which keywords your business should be dominating is a crucial part of online marketing. Some online marketing companies will guarantee you results fast, but they may choose keywords that they find easy to rank, rather than those that are best for your business.

So what makes a good key word or phrase? Quite simply, the words you want to dominate are the words your ideal clients and prospects are using right now, to search for you.

The quality of the keywords directly affects the quality of traffic to your site. SEO is not just about driving traffic, but driving traffic that wants your product or service - that of your 'ideal client'

When you know what search terms (keywords) your ideal client uses to look for services like yours, you will

be attracting prospects who:
- want your services
- are ready to buy from you
- are much easier to convert to clients

At EBS Digital, we generally spend the first 2 to 3 weeks of any SEO campaign making a detailed study of your website, your business and your industry. Once we understand your priority products and services and your ideal client, we then research a comprehensive list of keywords.

You can research keywords yourself and these keywords should:

a. Target people who want what your business provides

A good place to start when compiling your list is with the information we looked at in section 2 - your ideal client profile, the list of hot buttons, and the innovations that your business provides. If your company specializes in a certain geographical area, that area is a good one to include in some of your search terms. If you are a dentist in Boston, for instance, you may find it easier to rank for search terms that include Boston, or even the local area within the city you work in, like Newton or Chestnut Hill.

b. Your keywords should have reasonable to high search volume

Having decided your ideal search terms, you need to check whether anyone actually uses them to search online. You want terms which have reasonable search volume as it is this volume (or a good part of it) that you want to come to your website. If only 10 people per month search on a term you are considering, that term may rank high easily, but the benefit to your site traffic will be minimal.

c. Your keywords should be feasible to attain within a period of months.

Conversely, if you choose terms that have 5 million searches a month, you may not be able to optimize them efficiently or well. When we do keyword analyses, we list the volume of searches but also the Google competition, so we can see how feasible it is for us to get a good ranking for our clients on that term. If you are looking at searches with very high competition against high profile companies, you may need to consider your true niche and the value you deliver to your ideal clients and narrow down the keywords, perhaps using longer tail phrases which still have good volume and are more targeted to get you the prospects you want.

Long tail keywords are longer phrases that contain your keywords. If you are targeting people who want your legal services then you may also be targeting 'affordable legal services', 'Newton family lawyers', 'Divorce lawyers Boston' and so on. Each of those are long-tail keywords. These won't get as many searches as the word 'lawyer' alone, but they are less competitive because they are more specific. It also helps to qualify your traffic so you do not get traffic from people in Arizona who could never use your services anyway.

Here are some questions you can use when brain-storming your list:

- What keywords and keyword phrases would not only send you traffic, but qualified buyers?
- What are the keywords buyers would use for each of the products or services that you offer?
- What is the problem that your product or service is solving?
- Where is your business located?
- Where is your audience located?What are all the different synonyms for the words that you have come up with?

When you have done all this, you can also try some free keyword tools that can help you brainstorm different variations. Examples of keyword tools that you can easily find online are:

1. WordTracker
2. Keyword Discovery
3. Google Adwords
4. Wordze
5. Google Trends
6. Keyword Spy
7. MSN

Most are free and some may require a small payment. With these tools you can enter your chosen keywords into the search field and most of the links will generate key phrases for each of the terms you input. Google will give you synonyms as well, which will further help build your list.

These sites then help in evaluating the value and competition rate of each keyword.

Once you have a comprehensive list that includes the search volume for each keyword or phrase, transfer it to an Excel sheet or a list that you can keep to hand. Excel is easy to sort, because you should then sort your choices into different groups according to topic. For instance our builder would sort all his building service keywords into one group, and his supply keywords into another. This will also help you when you come to embed keywords on the correct web pages later on in the SEO process.

Next, it is a good idea to prioritize the keywords in each group. This keeps your SEO efforts organized; otherwise it is easy to start ranking your site for lower priority keywords. The top keywords in each group are the ones you will want to rank for. Lastly, you need to prioritize your groups and decide which are the most important to try and rank for.

On Page Optimization

Once you have selected and analyzed your keywords for appropriateness and feasibility, you can move on to actual optimization. Your first focus should be 'on page' optimization, which basically ensures your site itself is perfectly set up for search engine crawlers to find it and extract the correct information from its pages to help it rank.

Our on page work begins with an extremely thorough Site Evaluation and Analysis and I recommend you take the time to do the same for your site if you are implementing SEO yourself. The main elements to check are:

a. Site Structure & Navigation
b. URL Patterns
c. Tags
d. Site Maps & Robot.txt
e. Load Time
f. Error Pages
g. Content

Below we will look at each of these in more detail, so you know what to look for and what the ideal state should be.

a. Site Structure and Navigation

A good site structure helps people navigate your website but it also helps search engines find and index your content. Good site structure should:

• **Resemble a pyramid.** No section should be more than twice as large as any other section. Your site should not have too many main sections or an excessive number of sub-sections. There are online mapping tools like Gliffy to map your site, or you can sketch it out with pen and paper.

- **Organize your content**. Your site structure should organize your content and group it into sections so it is logical for visitors and search engines.
- **Link your content**. Inter-linking your content from one page to another helps rankings as well.

b. URL Patterns

The URL of each page (the address which appears at the top of your browser when you are on that page) should ideally be static and not dynamic. Each page on your website should have a unique URL. Each URL should describe the content of that page, yet it should be as short as possible. Include important keywords in your URL if possible.

c. Tags

Sorting out all the tags that are applied to your site pages is not an exciting job but it is essential. Before you start working on your tags, it is a good idea to have decided which pages are the best for which products or services that you provide. Once you have identified the best landing pages for each topic, you can go ahead and optimize using the most relevant and high priority keywords from your list.

Title Tags:

Title tags are important because search engines use the text within the title tag to determine what the content of the page is about. Limit your title tag to 65 characters or less (search engines don't display more). Try to create unique title tags for each page of your website that focus on a single core, relevant keyword that matches the theme of the page. If you are using a CMS like WordPress, you can install a plugin that lets you customize your title tags.

Meta Description Tags

Meta description tags summarize what your Web page content is about and they are displayed in bold as part of the information people see on a search engine results page.

Search engines look at meta tags to learn more about what the page is about. Write a brief yet informative description about your content, including the keyword or phrase used in the title tag.

Meta tags don't quite have the level of SEO importance they used to, but they are still very important. At one time, certain sites used meta tags to increase their rankings by including far too many keywords. Now search engines give more weight to inbound links and page content for ranking instead. But they still play an important role in an SEO strategy so do use them on all of your pages.

If you are wondering where your meta tags are, most content management systems let you easily edit meta tags without coding knowledge. If you don't have an editor, you can simply open a web page file (ending in .htm, .html, .asp or .php) in Notepad or a plain text editor and the meta tags will be found near the top of the document.

Keyword Tag:

This is not used by all search engines (at the time of writing, Yahoo! still uses it) but if you use this tag, try to use keyword phrases most relevant to the page involved. The number should not exceed 8-10 keywords except for the "Home Page".

Image/ ALT Tags:

Search engine spiders cannot read images that you place on your pages. Therefore you need to use <alt> image tags to describe your images. The <alt> tag should describe the image and be two to five words long and should ideally be based on one of your suitable keywords.

Make sure that your image is properly named with real words rather than a jumble of numbers and then add a title to describe the image. The title can be a bit longer than the <alt> tag and read like a sentence.

Relevant captions under or near images help the search engines and may produce slightly higher rankings.

Header Tags:

Main topics and ideas can be placed within header tags. They alter the format of the text in the Web browser and tell the search engines that these keywords and phrases are important. Header tags are arranged in preset levels of importance from <H1> to <H6>. Text included in an <H1> tag appears larger than other text on the page. Header tags can be used anywhere within the body of the text and only one H1 tag should exist on a page.

d. Site Maps & Robots.txt

If you do not have an XML site map, I highly recommend that you get one, because linking all the pages in your website to your site map ensures search engines will index and follow links in your site map. This can help you get new pages quickly ranked into search engine result pages.

An XML site map is simply an .xml file with a list of all your pages and when they were updated.

You can find site map generators online that will create the .xml file for you. Once you get the .xml file, simply upload it to the root directory of your website (e.g. www.website.com/sitemap.xml).

If your website is updated regularly, make it a good practice to update your xml file at least once a month so search engines have the freshest data.

Adding an XML site map is a component that is often overlooked. It may not make or break your SEO results but it can certainly help.

A robots file is a .txt file that blocks all unwanted folders and URLs from the search engine crawlers. You need a robots.txt file only if your site includes content that you don't want search engines to index. You can allow access to web content and disallow access to cgi, private and temporary directories, by creating a special file in the root of each server called "robots.txt". Google's Webmaster tools can help you generate a robots.txt file or you can manually create one with rules for which files to allow and disallow.

e. Load Time

Google has officially made loading time a factor in their rankings. In addition, slow loading speeds can turn people away from your site as we get more and more accustomed to moving across the internet very quickly. Causes of slow site speeds can be running a lot of video (hosting via a service like Easy Video, or embedding from YouTube can assist), or your cache, which can be optimized using plug ins like W3 Total Cache.

f. Error Pages

You may have at some time clicked on a website link that went nowhere. Often, you'll see a "404 message" or "Page Not Found." This usually happens when a page is moved to a new URL and the old link hasn't been directed to the new page.

Effective 404 error pages communicate why a particular page couldn't be displayed and what users can do next. Having that message can prevent you losing site visitors who may otherwise click back or away. If you choose to move a page on your website entirely, make certain that you use a permanent 301 redirect, a method used to change an old URL to a new one. Permanent 301 redirects are also important for SEO so search engines know where to find the page that was moved.

An orphan is a page with few or no links from other pages. It is also good to minimize the orphan pages on your site with some links to other relevant content pages.

g. Content

Speaking of content-linking internally brings us to page content optimization. When interlinking content, it is a good strategy to hyperlink content using the keywords when possible. When we implement 'on page' SEO at EBS Digital, we also often re-write or add content (with client approval) to websites that we optimize to embed keywords in a natural way.

Search engines like to see written content on the pages that people see but again, it is good to have determined the best landing pages to better target your keywords. Most importantly, you do not want to send people who have searched for one product line to a page that focuses on another line, or to a generic page. If searchers do not immediately find content that aligns with their expectation, they tend to leave.

Pick a primary keyword for each page and focus on optimizing that page for that word. Include the keywords in the body content but don't use them out of context and make sure they are relevant with the rest of your content. If you oversaturate a page with too many keywords, the page will lose its importance and authority.

Try to take a step back when you are wearing your SEO hat because it is easy to forget that we are writing and producing our websites for people first and for search engines second. Always prepare your content for your audience and then look at how to make it work for search engines. If you write this way round your text will feel natural and usually, what feels natural to people also works well for the search engines.

Your top keywords need to appear in your copy on a frequent basis. In the early days of SEO, pages were often 'stuffed' with keywords and the search engines caught on. Keyword density is now factored into the algorithms.

The best guide to an acceptable density of keywords is whether your copy sounds natural to most visitors. For example, which sounds the most natural to you?

1. EBS Digital provides ethical and effective SEO to help drive traffic and leads to your site with high quality optimization.

2. EBS Digital is a top SEO company providing SEO services for ethical SEO for SEO for the UK, SEO for the US and SEO for all your marketing and search engine needs.

So place a few of your keywords in bold on the page - but only once or twice. Search engine spiders also notice bold text, but it should not be overused.

Google's algorithms have recently been updated to include synonyms so you can use synonyms for your keyword to make your copy flow more naturally.

Before you move on with your on page optimization, please take some time to install Google Analytics. It is a free program that generates detailed statistics and information about your site's users, how long they stay, where they came from, their demographics, which pages they use, and which they bounce from.

There are multiple videos online that show you how to install Google Analytics and it is important to take the HTML tracking code it generates and place it into the source code of each page of your website.

Then set aside some time once a month at least to analyze your traffic data. Google Analytics will help you:

- improve content
- write better-targeted ads
- create a higher converting site
- find out where people are coming from
- find out where they tend to leave from
  You will be able to tell if a particular social media site

like Facebook is working well in driving prospects to your site, or which search terms are working well on Google.

You can also adjust the pages that have high exit counts to try and lower the number of people leaving.

Tracking and metrics are an amazing feature of online marketing and they are almost real time in many instances, so there is no need to wait weeks and months to find out if your marketing spend is working. A poorly performing ad can be tweaked, the landing page adjusted and the whole campaign pulled or re-calibrated within days, or even hours.

3. Off Page Optimization

So you have put in some time targeting the correct keywords for the visitors you want to attract, and you have probably spent many hours working on making sure your site code and content are at optimal levels.

Now it is time for the third stage of search engine optimization - off page optimization. This includes:

a. Link building
b. Directory submissions
c. Production and posting of fresh content (articles, press releases and blogs)

a. Link Building

One of the major indicators to a search engine that your site is an authority in your field is the quality and number of incoming links. It makes a large difference to your SEO ranking and, while we include link-building in our SEO packages, it is one of the reasons we frequently recommend that our SEO clients supplement their general optimization with our specialized link building packages.

Incoming links are those that point to your site from other websites or blogs. These links lead to a page within your site. Each link acts as "vote" of confidence or trust in your website content. The more votes you have, the more authority your site will have on your specific topic. As your authority increases, so will your page rank.

If your website is filled with high quality content that is of value to your audience, you will naturally earn incoming links over time because other websites will want to direct their users to you.

Of course, like all SEO strategies, even proactive link building takes some time because you first need to collect the links and then allow time for search engine spiders to crawl your site. And, like all SEO strategies, there is always the temptation to take short cuts and try to work around the system. It doesn't work, so try and avoid offers of links that seem too good to be true because they undoubtedly will be. Search engines are also suspicious if you get 1000 links overnight and that strategy does not have as much impact as building 5 meaningful links per day for 20 days.

So, to increase your page ranking, you need to increase the volume of links that point to your site but also, those links should be from pages with high perceived authority, because not all links are equal.

The criteria that search engines use to determine a website's value is highly complex, and is not fully shared with the general public or webmasters.

Generally, a well-established website that is a known expert on a particular topic carries more weight than a newly established blog on the same topic. The linking site's authority is passed on to your site. For your link building, you want to be targeting the expert websites to get the most from your efforts.

Remember to gather links that point to a variety of pages on your website to diversify your page rank options. If you have specific pages on specific topics, create a mini link building campaign for each topic to better your chances of ranking for your target keywords. Avoid linking only to your home page.

Link building strategies:

Link building tactics can be complex but there are some relatively simple strategies you can use if you can allocate some time.

Remember that you always want to be aiming for links from sites that are relevant to what you do. Links from sites that are not related to what your site or your business is about will not help your rankings. The best strategy is to always provide quality content that people care about.

1. Get links from commenting on blogs

Most blog platforms offer the option for readers to post comments. When a comment is posted, so is your name and website address. This counts as a link, and may drive some traffic to your site via the blog owner and other readers. I would suggest the following caveats, which hold true for all online marketing because following them helps you focus on authenticity rather than self-promotion for its own sake:
- Write good comments that respond and contribute to the subject matter in the post
- If you don't have anything fresh to say it's better to wait till another post
- Don't use your comments to promote your site

2. Ask your colleagues and business contacts for links

Start with your circle of colleagues, partners and distributors and ask them to link to your website, assuming that the links make sense to your keywords and general website topics.

Some websites have pages dedicated to the web pages of other businesses that they recommend, so investigate and see if you can be added to these pages.

3. Ask for links from bloggers and webmasters

The most popular websites get hundreds of these requests every day and most end up ignored.

However, if there are sites or good blogs related to your industry, consider contacting the webmaster and asking for a link. Keep your email requests short and to the point and include a good reason why the link makes sense.

4. Link Bait

Link bait always sounds like a slightly shady strategy from the title, but if it is done with the intention to provide highly engaging or entertaining content, it should be a very good strategy that encourages people to link to that content or share it through social networks precisely because it is good.

Often, link bait has relevance to current events or trends and ignites a discussion or comment. Examples of effective content include lists ('My top ten ways to..' or 'The 5 best...') and is easy to scan through. These are all types of content that people like to link to, but do be sure that what you try works with the tone of your brand and your business:

Humor: Something clever that makes people laugh is going to get passed on quickly.
Controversy: Can spur discussion but it can easily back fire and cast your site in a poor light.
Valuable Content: Compiling lists of advice, information, news or product reviews is an effective way to draw people to your site.
Images: Images that tell a story work well. Re-captioning a news photo is an example.
Interviews: Think about people who are opinion leaders or highly successful in your industry. What would your audience want to know about them? What kind of messages could they provide your audience with?

Giveaways: Pair up with a complementary business and offer a giveaway through your site. The participating business benefits from the exposure, and your site benefits from increased traffic and links pointing to your giveaway site or post.

Sneak Peeks: an inside track on a new product or service related to your industry brings links (e.g. if you are a dentist with a view on the latest whitening product).

Link Building Strategies to Avoid:

Buying and selling links: Search engines tend to penalize sites that broker links, as well as the websites that use their services.

Joining link networks: Groups of sites that are questionable may offer to spread your link text and URL out to their many sites in exchange for a link from you. Generally you will be exchanging with nothing but poor quality and bad associations.

b. Directory Promotion

There are hundreds of thousands of directories online and you do not need to be in all of them. Starting locally is a good idea; your local Chamber of Commerce, business associations, the Better Business Bureau and neighborhood associations. Each of these organizations should have a website with members' businesses listed.

Secondly, if you are a part of any industry associations be sure to register your business with their listings service or consider joining some associations.

There are also many free and paid directories available online such as:

Open Directory Project
Best of the Web
Yahoo! Directory
Yellow Pages

US Chamber of Commerce
US Better Business Bureau
MSN (Bing)
Yelp
City Search

All of these submissions, if done consistently, bring in more qualified back links and traffic to your website. We implement these activities on a monthly basis for our clients and you should do the same for your site as continual, constant attention to all of the off page work will build a consistent result for your site's rankings and authority.

c. Production and posting of fresh content

This is the final part of off-page optimization. Content that changes often includes articles, blog postings and press releases. Again, there are online directories and sites specifically for you to post articles and press releases.

By the time you reach this stage, you will have done a lot of research and have a very clear picture of your ideal client, their wants and desires, and how you can best meet those desires.

If your interests and passions match those of your target audience, it will be much easier for you to make the kind of real connections that define a more authentic online interaction today.

However excited you are about your business or your field of expertise, it can be hard to set aside time to produce the level of content that makes a difference to your business and there are times when just generating that content feels like a lot of work.

Here are some ways to make producing your ongoing content more of a system that allows you enjoy the process rather than a random and rushed exercise. Start off with four questions:

1. Who will be interested in this content?
2. What questions does this content answer for them?
3. What keywords will be used to find it?
4. What do you want the audience to do after consuming it (what is the call-to-action)?

Find a topic where you and your expertise or passion fills the gap. Your keyword research provided you with insights as to what your audience is using to search online. Google Insights can help you to find out just how popular your topic is and where there may be pockets of intense interest.

You do not need a topic that everyone is searching, just one that resonates with your audience.

Next, look for any content "gaps" that you can fill with your particular knowledge or viewpoint. If you can be a big fish in a small content pond, it helps your online marketing, and looking at your niche market and your own innovations in your business is a good place to start brainstorming for these gaps.

Invest time in research. Use AllTop.com to find heavily trafficked blogs covering your subject area. See what is making news in Google News, Topix, Yahoo! News and Blog Pulse. Once you have research in place, you can set up a plan to produce content.

Write down all your content ideas and include ideas you know you will enjoy writing or recording.

Content is not just long text articles. Other examples could be:

• Short articles
• Press releases for new products or services
• Profiles
• Opinion pieces
• Audio podcasts
• Videos
• Images

Also, feel free to circulate blog content or other people's

relevant videos or articles and if you can add your own unique viewpoint to them, that also works well. Use news stories to populate your Facebook feed, Twitter feed or as inspiration for a blog post.

You can also ask people you know - clients, suppliers, employees - to contribute, and try to give them a topic or guidelines so you keep a coherent tone and plan.

You can also use the same content in multiple ways on multiple platforms in multiple channels. For example, a photo can be posted to Flickr, sent to Twitter, pulled into the sidebar of your website, shared on Facebook, added to an e-book and so on.

How do I organize all this?

An editorial calendar is an excellent way to organize your ideas and develop a publishing schedule. It takes a little time up front but once you have it, you have a process to refer to that helps prevent oversights and last minute panics and makes your entire strategy coherent and professional. Try to plot out a calendar for content, with responsibilities and deadlines, for the first six weeks of your project and refresh it at the beginning of every month.

Most importantly, set aside 30 to 60 minutes each week to write about your business. Don't be concerned about the quality at first or having it in a set format. It is a good idea to brainstorm anything and everything from your goals and vision to service and product descriptions, points of difference, your elevator pitch and so on. Think about current trends in your industry, or how your product or service relates to what is going on in the news. You will be surprised at how much you can pull from these to develop into articles and blog posts, and how much you can use for social media marketing (which we will cover in a later chapter).

Search Engine Optimization - Ongoing Maintenance

This last chapter should have given you a little insight into the many facets of good SEO. It might also have felt like a lot of work. It is, but it is doable, especially if you can be consistent and disciplined in your approach.

Once you have completed all of the above steps, you do need to set aside some time weekly to maintain and continue your efforts otherwise you will see your hard-earned rankings start to slip back as this is an ongoing process whether you do it in house or whether you outsource that service.

1. You will want to keep tracking your rankings in the major search engines, based on the targeted keywords. We issue monthly reports for our clients that show the upward trend (as well as reports on all that month's submissions and social bookmarking) and you can run similar reports using online tools.

2. Re-optimization or tweaking of the site pages, covering the optimization steps noted above, is needed regularly to improve and/or retain the top rankings.

3. Search engines keep updating their algorithms and you can subscribe to receive constant updates on such changes. Based on these, you can schedule a regular re-evaluation to help keep your site free of search engine incompatibility issues.

4. Google Analytics is a great resource for tracking your increasing site traffic and also to see which pages people spend most time on, which ones they leave quickly, and where prospects are coming to you from and using which keywords.

5. Some keywords lose popularity due to seasonal changes, market issues or world events. Your products

and services may change and so might your target market. Re-visiting your keywords every couple of months and refining and replacing any that do not work for you anymore with extra research will ensure that your site is always targeting the optimal keywords for your business.

6. You may need copywriting revisions based on any new keywords - if you do decide to target a new keyword or phrase, you will need to adjust some of your relevant site copy to reflect the new addition.

7. Link-building strategies and content creation and posting should always be ongoing as part of your online marketing.

Making sure that your business achieves strong visibility takes dedication, perseverance, in depth knowledge and some clear, detailed and easy to implement systems. If you do decide you want to hire experts to do all this for you, then this chapter should have given you a good idea of what to ask them, and some tools with which to manage their work.

At the end of an intense chapter of information like this, I would suggest that you take a moment to write down between 3 and 5 goals for your online marketing.

The idea is to narrow down from the plethora of information you have just taken in and to focus on why online marketing is a good idea for your business.

Examples of goals:

- Set up my first website!
- Increase leads to my site by 10%
- Build a mailing list of 10,000 people
- Get onto page 1 of Google for 5 key search terms

Then you can go back and apply the most relevant information from this section and create a manageable plan to take your site to the top of the search engines, drive revenue and convert it to sales.

PPC

Pay-per-click advertising is just what it sounds like - advertising that is charged based on how many people click on the ad involved. Generally, PPC advertising refers to the paid search and sponsored listings that appear in search results (usually on the right hand side of the page) or on websites as sponsored links or partner ads.

Using billboards or TV ads might be far out of range for most small businesses, and your message goes in front of a lot of people who are completely uninterested in your products. But PPC ad campaigns can be strictly budgeted and targeted. They also build on the work you have already done to optimize your website for search engines, as they are usually based on the same keywords. They are also easy to create without the help of a designer, because they are text based.

If some of your ideal keywords are very competitive, and your business can't easily make it to page 1, PPC ads offer you an opportunity to get your business seen in areas that might otherwise be overlooked.

PPC campaigns are run via an account with one of the main search engines, and are displayed based on a group of keywords and per-click bids. Then, the search engine displays the ads that are most relevant to the search query in order of the highest bid.

If that sounds complex, it is. The search engines use an algorithm to determine which ads will appear, when and how often. Relevance is determined based on the keyword groups associated with each ad, as well as the ad copy itself and the content on the web page the ad points to. Bids vary depending on how many people are vying for the same keyword, as well as factors like the time of day, week or season.

PPC campaigns can offer some of the best value for money when it comes to getting your message out to the people who need to see it. However, there are potential pitfalls that can lose you money as well.

Potential PPC Pitfalls

Like every other marketing strategy, PPC works better for some businesses than for others. On the whole, PPC can work well, but monitoring constantly is absolutely key, along with consistency in making tweaks and changes as required.

Here are some of the potential drawbacks you should be aware of:

Is your website lacking?

The best PPC ads and management can't help you make sales without back up from an effective website or landing page. Effective websites are well written and well designed, directly relate to the ad and have a strong call to action (please see earlier in this section for guidelines on websites and landing pages).

Do your keywords have low search volumes?

This can happen if your niche market is too small. Try expanding your keyword list and evaluate the results.

Are you starting it and ignoring it?

PPC campaigns do not and should not run on their own. They need to be managed all the time, as bids and search volumes change. You should be checking on them at least once a day, at the start of your campaigns. You should also be looking at your analytics to determine which are your highest performing keywords and adjusting your PPC accordingly.

Just in case that has put you off PPC, here are some benefits:

PPC Benefits

1. PPC is highly targeted. Choosing the right keywords gives you access directly to your ideal prospects.

2. Metrics are available 24/7. Almost immediately, you can see and track and monitor your results, and not only the cost per click (CPC) but also the clicks-to-impression ratio (CTR), total impressions and total ad spend. Reading these will help you decide how to adjust your ad strategy.

3. You are in control. If your keywords don't have enough traffic, you can change them with new ones. If you are not happy with your budget, you can reduce it or increase it with a mouse click. If your ad copy needs adjusting, you can do it at once.

There are many places to advertise but the best known is Google, with Google AdWords.

Google's advertising services are clear and sophisticated. Google has by far the highest search volumes of any of the search engines.

Half of respondents to the UK SEM Report 2007 said they were getting an ROI of over 300% for PPC, and just under a third reported an ROI of over 500%.

Returns like that need constant monitoring and management to achieve. To give you an example, when we set up a PPC campaign at Enlightenment, we implement the following steps and these can form a good guideline for your own managed campaign:

1. Be clear on your Ideal Client – By now, you should have a clear idea of the clients and prospects who love your services and products, who buy often and refer often.

These are the people you want to target.

2. Create your Google AdWords account and follow the steps for creating your profile. You can use your existing Google account to do this, or create a new one.

3. Keyword Research – you need to prepare a list of core keywords that best describe your business, products or services and attract your ideal clients. Once you have a list, try and refine it to focus on those that offer the least competition with the highest search volume. Then, compile lists separated into specific product or service groups upon which you can create campaigns. It is not unlike the process you follow to come up with your SEO keywords. Once you have an organized set of words you can begin to assign groups of keywords to individual ads. Each campaign you set up will generally have a series of ad groups within it and each ad group has a set of ads.

For example, you could assign an ad group to each product that you sell, and then you could allocate a small group of keywords to each group. Let's look at a business that sells lighting:

Product	Keyword Group
Table Lamps	table lamp, table lamps, bedside lights, table lights, bedside lamps, lamp shades
Desk Lamps	desk lamps, desk lighting, office lamps, desk spotlight
Ceiling Lights	ceiling lights, wall lights, spot lights, pendant lights, recessed lighting, ceiling lighting

This is a small sample to give you an idea, but it is a good idea to limit your keywords per group to no more than 20 or 30 - it tends to keep more relevancy as the keywords are more targeted.

4. Placement analysis – make yourself a list of costs and pricing for top placement on Google Adwords, Yahoo! Search Marketing and other search engines for your target phrases and appropriate combinations.

5. Set up match types. Google and the other engines offer at least three match types:

- Broad matches work well for long-tail keywords and for words that are often spelled poorly. Your ads tend to appear more because there are many different options for matching.
- Exact matches work best for shorter keywords and they make it easier to control your spend.
- Negative matches tell Google that you do not want your ad to appear next to a particular keyword such as 'used' or 'discount'. It refines your targeting to filter out less than ideal clients for you.

6. Set your budget - think about the budget you want to spend, bearing in mind that the first time you use PPC can involve a period of tweaking and adjustment to produce better and better returns on investment. Start by asking yourself the following questions:

- Why am I using PPC? To drive sales or just get more traffic/leads?
- What amount makes sense to spend for each sale, or lead?
- Which products or services do I want to promote most?
- Is there a seasonal or cyclical aspect to my sales?

If you sell DVDs at $15 you will be spending much

less per sale than if you are selling a $10,000 item.

When you have decided your total PPC budget, you can further allocate sections of your budget to each ad group.

7. Manage your bidding – clearly, your aim is to bid on keywords that deliver the best return on investment and conversions.

Bid management can get quite complicated and there are a few different ways you can bid in Google AdWords:

a) Maximum CPC Bidding - the standard setting. You decide what the maximum cost per click is that you are willing to spend and based on that, Google displays your ad until your budget is reached and then your campaign stops until you authorize more payment.

b) Budget Optimizer - this is a low maintenance option where you set a budget and a timescale (usually a month) and Google tries to get you as many clicks as possible within that month.

c) Automatic Bidding - Here, Google allows you to set an average dollar amount that you are happy to pay for each click, then manages your bids with that figure as the target.

When selecting your keywords, Google shows estimated search volumes and the average Cost Per Click for each keyword.

The CPC is calculated based on algorithms that determine relevancy. Three things should be relevant to each other when you set up a PPC campaign:

- your chosen keywords
- your ad copy - this should relate to your keywords
- your landing page (or destination URL) - should include your keywords.

If they do not match well, Google sees the ad as less relevant and may show it less.

No two PPC campaigns are the same, and so there is no formula for allocating your budget except to monitor your costs and to focus on the ad groups or campaign keywords that are converting well for you.

8. Write good ads – compelling ad copy is crucial to your campaign. People scan and decide to click or not to click extremely quickly. Effective ad copy attracts or interrupts, informs and, most importantly, converts to clicks and sales. These are the main components of your PPC ad copy:

Headline - the PPC headline is short (usually 25 characters only) and should contain keywords. For keyword-targeted ad campaigns, the keywords are more important than the attractiveness of the headline. Try using questions in your headline to inspire curiosity or some kind of call to action. 'Get an instant building quote' works better than than 'We provide quotes'

Body Copy - two lines of body copy is standard. Benefits and stand out features should dominate. Try using a benefit in the first line and a feature in the second. Try to choose a big benefit - the major way in which your product is going to improve your prospects' lives. Find the most important, most valuable benefit that you worked on when you innovated your business using the earlier section of this book, and describe it in the first line.

Display URL - the web address that people see. It should contain keywords to encourage click throughs. For instance www.desklamps.com.

Destination URL - This is the site page or landing page that the visitor will reach after they click the ad. This will be the URL that search engine crawlers use to determine how relevant your ad is. Make sure that these match, or are relevant to each other.

Ultimately, your ads should let searchers know that you

have the answers they want. Keywords are very important because they appear in bold in search listings which helps your ad stand out and be noticed.

9. Track and analyze – Using Google Adwords helps you to produce and analyze periodic reports that provide your ROI rate as the campaign proceeds and it is important to stay on top of your ad performance to avoid money draining away unnecessarily.

An excellent tool is split A/B testing. Simply, you run two ads that have only one small difference, and you compare the results to see which one is more effective. Some of the things you can split test are:

Headlines
Capitalization
Display URL
Destination URL
Dynamic headlines or ad copy

But do change only one thing at a time so that you can easily tell which variable makes the difference.

In terms of analyzing overall performance of your campaign, here are 3 metrics to keep an eye on:

- Click-Through-Rate (CTR): This refers to the ratio of clicks (the number of people who clicked the ad) to impressions (the number of people who saw it).
- Cost Per Click (CPC): The average cost per click will be displayed for each ad you run. Cross check that against your click throughs to check whether you are paying too much for keywords.
- Conversion Rate: You can decide what constitutes a conversion for you - sales or sign ups for instance - and then you can more easily tell which ads are converting and which are underperforming.

10. Adjust and Tweak - You can start tweaking early. Decide whether you want to get a sample of 100 or 1000 clicks (it will vary according to your industry and how many clicks you are getting per day). It is useful to decide a number in your mind and when you reach it, take some time to analyze the metrics above. Based on the results you can:

- Increase your spending - if the ad is doing well.
- Decrease your spending - if performance is underwhelming but you feel there are ways you can try to turn it around and you need time to do so.
- Stop your spending - if your results are poor or if you are uncertain, it is simple to pause a campaign or delete it and start again.

Extra tips to maximize your campaign:

1. Geo-target - you don't have to have a physical location to run ads targeted at a certain area or city but you can choose to have your ad only display to people who are within a certain area. It helps reduce competition for the keywords. Also, if you are a builder who likes to work close to home, you can choose to only display ads within 10 miles of your house.

Viewers are also more likely to click ads that mention their geographic area, so when you geo-target, use the place name in your ad. The landing page the ad leads to should also have some relevance to the geographic area so you should consider adding some local keywords to the landing page. You can then measure the results against your other, keyword-based campaigns and if this is profitable, compare campaigns between different geographic locations.

2. Placement-target - these campaigns use websites instead of keywords to display your ads with Google's content network. Webmasters can choose to display a box of Google ads on their website or blog and earn money each time a reader clicks an ad. You can choose which websites you want your ad to appear on.

It is a little like traditional banner advertising. The advantages of placement targeting are the control you have over your ads, and exactly where they are displayed. Also, by choosing to have ads on high traffic sites, you benefit from someone else's traffic without having to generate it yourself.

Your research will be different. Your goal is to find relevant websites with a high page rank and clear AdSense ads.

The easiest way to find them (and it is still time-consuming) is to run a search on your top keywords and then write down the top URLs (organic search results and ad results) which feature Adsense ads in an Excel sheet.

Your ad copy for placement ads would be less dependent on keywords and can be more creative in interrupting your prospects and then engaging them.

3. Timed ads - if you know that there is a peak time for people to buy your products you can schedule your ads at a particular time using the scheduling tool in Google AdWords. You can pick a particular day or days to run ads on (or to avoid) and you can decide to pay more for ads at certain times of the day.

4. Consider Facebook ads - Facebook is a social network not a search engine, so it places ads based on demographic and psychographic information taken from their users' profiles. As long as your prospects are using Facebook (and nearly 800 million people are) it is an interesting strategy to consider. As with Google Ads, Facebook offers a CPC or CPM basis and they use an algorithm to show your ad to users who match the criteria you have selected. The personal demographics that you can choose from mean that the targeting is excellent.

What I've given you here is a good amount of detail that should help you get started and run a good PPC and indeed, a good SEO, campaign. Both require input, thought and then analysis to work well, which is why they are both often campaigns that our clients hand over to us to handle. It is always good to understand PPC, SEO and all aspects of online marketing thoroughly, but not always necessary to do everything yourself. You have to evaluate where you are in the growth of your business and whether you are in a position to spend your time in technical implementation and in depth analysis, or whether you want an experienced team to take that on for you.

Either ways, there are immense opportunities to drive traffic to your site but they will only do well if PPC and SEO are given their due time during the set up process and then given attention as they proceed.

There are other ways to drive traffic to your site and to your business, but perhaps none has taken off so exponentially during the last year or two, especially for small businesses, as social media marketing which is the topic we will look at in the next section.

Hanan Kattan

Section 3
Social Media

157

I think that most of us know by now that Facebook has 800 million users and growing. It is an often-quoted fact and an amazing one that reflects the speed and intensity with which our culture has changed over the past few years.

What I have been impressed by recently is the way that social media has been adopted by businesses and especially small to medium-sized businesses.

Social media use by small businesses doubled between 2009 and 2010.

Nearly 50% of small businesses have successfully connected with new customers using their social networks.

More than half of all Facebook and Twitter users say they are more likely to buy the brands of people and companies that they follow.

If you think that trends like this might not apply to you because your product or service targets an older audience, then you should also be aware that currently one of the the fastest growing segments on Facebook is 55-65 year old females.

I could go on with statistics but the point is clear for business owners - if you are not using social media on a consistent and comprehensive basis, you are deliberately cutting yourself off from a new and growing source of leads and clients.

As a society, we simply do not respond to direct mailings and traditional advertising as we once did. Now when we have questions, we go to Google, or to our social networks to find answers that we trust more. So it makes sense for your business to be ready to answer those questions that relate to your niche. Social media gives your business a unique opportunity to interact and build trust with your customers and potential customers.

The dry definition of social media is that it describes websites and software that allow members to post, bookmark, discuss, share and create content within a specific network. Members have profiles that contain selected information and they can decide who they want to include in their network.

The power of social media lies in speed and trust. If one person recommends a YouTube movie trailer on their Facebook page, and 20 of their friends watch it, and then 3 of those tweet about it to their 500 followers...you can see the ripple effect outward and how hundreds and then thousands of people can begin to spread that trailer like a virus, which is where we got the reference to viral marketing.

I experienced this immense power first hand with the first feature films that I produced, The World Unseen and I Can't Think Straight. They were well-received by audiences, winning over 30 awards internationally, but they had only modest theatrical releases. Despite that, the word-of-mouth reviews were excellent and passed from fan to fan like wildfire. Thousands of people created fan videos using footage and songs from the films. We kept the entire films off YouTube as much as we could, but we have gathered over 100 million hits to date on the trailers and related fan videos - a response I could not have dreamed of, even though I worked hard to produce fun and exciting video content to help create and continue interest in the films. We were blessed with the strong and continuous support from fans throughout the world and those numbers continue to grow daily through our social media interactions.

I think that a lot of the success was due to authenticity, which is an attribute I have talked about before. The content of the films, and the genuine dedication to their messages of integrity and honesty from myself and my partner Shamim, who wrote and directed them, all struck a chord with people who had enjoyed the stories.

Far from acting as a shield, interacting with people you have never met through social media actually demands a true and real interaction. Somehow, anything that is insincere or careless is noticed quickly.

Although many more companies today have a social media presence, a lot of them are still not sure how best to maximize it to help their businesses grow. As with all marketing, a strategy and overall plan is a good place to start.

When you involve your business in social media you need to do so in a strategic, well-thought out way. In this section, we will take a look at using social media for your business, and then I will look at some major networks:

- Facebook
- Twitter
- LinkedIn
- YouTube

Then we will take a look at how to produce and best use strategies and tactics like:

- Blogging
- Articles
- Podcasting
- Videos
- Press Releases

And finally, I'll suggest some ways to manage social media so that it does not take over your business life but becomes a regular and valuable part of it.

There is much more to the realm of social media - many more networks and many more strategies. It is a world that moves quickly, but my aim here is to give an overview that will concentrate on basic principles. For updated details, there are a host of streams and blogs that will keep you on top of things daily. One that I like a lot is Social Media Examiner.

We also update our EBS Digital newsletter regularly with important social media and online marketing updates.

Benefits of Social Media for Business

Social media marketing is about creating, building and nurturing relationships. As with any good reciprocal relationship, social media asks that you listen first and respond afterwards. Listening to your customers (and potential customers) gives you a first hand sense of what they like and don't like about your business, or about products and services similar to yours. This gives you a unique chance to innovate and innovation is the best way to separate your business from the others in your field so that you begin to serve a new niche, as we discovered in the first section of this book.

Listening to your clients and prospects and showing them that you understand is appreciated by social media users, just as we appreciate those traits in our face to face interactions with our loved ones and friends. Using social media in your business allows you to:

- Be more accessible to customers for feedback, service and general communication
- Build trust
- Become an authority in your niche market
- Hold dialogues that can evolve and produce new services and products. Clients and prospects tend to be more informal and open on social networks than in more traditional business interactions
- Build excitement and anticipation around your products or services
- Show clients more of your behind-the-scenes life and the way you work if that would interest them and excite them more about your business (this works well in the entertainment industry and sports industries for instance)
- Build your brand at a grass roots level

If you are just now thinking about setting up a social media presence for your business, you can start by considering where your ideal customers and online audience are likely to be interacting with each other and with you.

If you have taken the time to look at your demographics, then that is a very good place to start. If you have worked through your psychographics and figured out your niche market, that is even better, because you will have a very good sense of the answers to these questions:

- How old is my audience?
- What do they do for a living?
- What are they passionate about?
- What do they look for in social media sites - social chat, advice, opinions?
- Based on that, which sites are they using most?

If you spend time on Twitter, Facebook and LinkedIn looking up topics related to your business you will start to get an idea of what kind of pages and groups are out there that relate to you, their size and the level of participation they receive.

Google Groups lets you run searches for your product, service or industry. You may find discussion forums that give you some insight into what people are talking about and thinking. Digg has similar search features that are good for research.

Spend some time in and around these communities until you get a sense for what they are about, and how they use the network and then you can consider how your business fits in or, ideally, enhances the discussion because of your unique perspective and/or innovations.

Your social media messages are a less formal extension of your core marketing messages, so it is important to keep your innovations and benefits in mind and to plan some goals that form the basis for your social media actions.

While social networks are largely informal, remember that you are still representing your business to a large network so you need to be strategic about how you interact.

This leads to your business's personality online. The tone and manner in which you post make a difference to the way you are perceived. Are your blogs funny, quirky, informative or factual? Are your comments or responses to customers chirpy and witty or more structured? Some of this will depend on who your customers are, but what really matters is that your personality online is congruent with your personality off line.

If your company trades on an air of reliability and solidity, do not undermine that with quirky observations that could alienate. Similarly, if you target a young, tech-savvy demographic, posting long, dense, text content might not be as useful as producing quick, sharp videos.

The good news is that most of this is common sense. Be consistent with your business and the brand you have created and want to continue to build.

The next question is - where do you build those networks for your business? Let's go through a few of the major platforms and players in the social media world currently. I will not go over how to set up accounts or join these sites, as they all make that very easy to do and many of you will already have accounts set up.

Social Media Platforms/Networks

Twitter

Twitter is a kind of micro-blog, a stream of short status updates limited to 140 characters. You set up an account and you receive a stream of posts from people you choose to follow.

Twitter is surprisingly good at creating a personality for your business. It is useful for posting frequent updates, announcing new products, linking to new blog posts, asking your audience questions and encouraging your customers to provide quick feedback.

Using Twitter for your business:

1. Follow people within your niche market, or in complementary or related areas. Do look at those businesses' feeds and be strategic about who you choose to follow. Often

when you follow someone, they will follow you back.

2. Keep your tweets valuable and professional. You don't need to offer your irritation with morning traffic or personal details on your business Twitter feed. Good ideas for tweets might be short insights you've had, links to articles you think are relevant, links to your blogs (or those of others) or links to a video or article about your business, or related to your business. As with all social media, people will evaluate your worth on the value of your content. If they open 5 tweets in a week from you and find 5 excellent pieces of content that help and inform them, they will regard you highly.

3. Use Twitter to link to special offers or new products, but make these infrequent links between other content.

4. Think about your audience first and your company second - this relates to points 2 & 3 above but is a good rule of thumb.

5. Use tweets to highlight your expertise by linking generously to content that educates. It will help position you as the expert so that people are ready to come to you when they need help in your field of expertise.

6. Twitter shortens links automatically and also makes it very simple to post photos, so consider using images as tweets as well.

You can sync your Twitter feed to your LinkedIn profile, to your blog page and to your Facebook profile. Usually it comes up as a short feed on the side of the page and it is another way to show movement and dynamism on those pages too.

Tweeting is easy to do on the move because updates are short. There are a host of apps including one from Twitter itself and TweetDeck which are optimized for mobiles and iPads. Personally, I love using Flipboard because it makes even the short tweets from my feed look like glossy magazine articles by opening and displaying the photos and articles posted by people that you are following.

Facebook

Facebook started in 2004 as a closed community for college students but has since expanded to become the second most popular site on earth (after Google). Over half of users in the US are aged 26 to 60. One in every eight minutes spent on the internet is spent on Facebook.

There are many Facebook statistics cited all the time, and with good reason. The sheer scale of Facebook is staggering according to its own published statistics. Of the 800 million users, nearly half a billon log in to the site on any given day. A quarter of a million photos are uploaded daily on Facebook, and the average number of connections for each user is 130.

Facebook has created this amazing presence by allowing and encouraging users to connect with each other and to share information in a variety of ways and it has evolved hugely in its applications for business users recently.

With Facebook, as with Twitter, my overview is just that - an overall look at the benefits of using these applications so that, if you haven't used them yet, you may feel inspired to do so, and if you are using them, you may get some ideas of how to make them work better for you. Benefits for having a company presence on Facebook are numerous and include:

- Building your brand and company culture
- Connecting and engaging with customers and potential customers
- Promoting marketing content including webinars, videos, blogs and so on
- Running offers and ideas past your community of clients/prospects

- Creating leads for your business

Page versus Profile:

When you use Facebook personally, you set up a profile. When you set up Facebook for your business you should be setting up a Page. A Page has more functionality that works for businesses than a standard profile:

- You can have more than one administrator which means that more than one person can help manage your account. You manage the account anonymously, behind your company's name. If your name is part of your branding because you have a profile, you can set up a Page in your name.
- Pages are public and can rank in Facebook searches and also in public search results.
- Pages have categories that can help you get listed in more relevant search results.
- Anyone can join your page, without waiting for you to accept them.

Starting a Page takes a matter of minutes. Of course, it is all about the content that you then put on the page to attract your ideal clients and prospects. Here are some other factors to help you make the most of your Facebook Page:

1. As an administrator of your Page, you can also be a fan and you can do that by clicking the "Like" button on your Page. Once you become a fan, you are listed amongst all the other fans on your Page, and all the Pages of which you are a fan will show up on your profile, giving your business more visibility to your network.

2. When you start gathering fans, don't forget to draw on your existing client base, email list or blog followers. Let them know that they can interact with you on Facebook. You can reach people by email, adding a link

to FB in your signature or placing a FB icon on your website and blog.

3. Facebook Pages have very good features like discussion boards and a YouTube video box which you can use to engage with your fans.

4. The news feed has immense viral opportunity in Facebook. When someone becomes a fan or adds a comment to your Page or interacts in some way, their activity is published to their own news feed which is seen by their friends, giving you a wide and extended audience.

5. Your Page is automatically made public (unless you choose for it not to be) so it can get indexed by search engines which gives you the opportunity to drive organic search traffic to your Page.

6. We discussed Facebook ads earlier, and these ads also allow you to advertise your own Facebook Pages and Events to gather more fans and followers. An excellent feature of Facebook ads is that you can place an image in them (unlike regular Google Ads). This can have a big impact on response rates.

7. Facebook also has a 'sponsored stories' ad type which lets you post items that have mentioned your business in an interesting or engaging way, and using this option lets you send that story out to people outside your core followers. Sponsored story ads tend to be more cost-effective than the standard ads.

8. Another good feature of Facebook ads is that you can target the ads to your connections. These could include people who are fans, people who are not your fans and, perhaps most useful of all, the friends of your fans. These are people who already have things in common with your fan base and who might therefore have a greater interest

in your product or service.

A big advantage with Facebook is that so many people use it so often, and so they are used to the interface and to visiting the site regularly. That means that they know instinctively where to find information and they find it easily which should make it easier for you as a business owner to demonstrate your profile and personality as a company. Even more effective, from the perspective of online marketing, is that the core purpose of Facebook is to connect and share. It hands you the opportunity to build a mutually satisfying relationship with your clients and prospects and fans. All you are required to do is spend some time getting your business ready to engage and then be prepared to measure and improve on the results you generate.

In most cases, Pages work best for businesses but once in a while, a Facebook Group makes sense instead of, or in addition to, your Page. Groups are meant for a community of people with a common interest, and they are a little more like a discussion forum, while a Page represents a brand or a company or a celebrity who has fans.

Another aspect of Facebook that you should be aware of is the marvelous technology that helps it supply timely and relevant information to its users. Facebook has its own algorithm, called EdgeRank.

EdgeRank determines which items are shown to a Facebook user in his or her news feed. Presenting every single activity or comment from every one of your fans or friends would lead to overwhelm, and so EdgeRank helps to decide which pieces of information might be the most useful or meaningful to you.

There have been complaints from users who dislike the idea that Facebook decides what matters to them, and who don't like the possibility that news that is several hours or more old is ranked above the very latest posts. I believe that Facebook gives strictly chronological access as well, beneath these sorted choices, so that is something to be aware of.

As a business you may ask, how does EdgeRank decide who and how many people will see my content or posts? What will give my content the 'edge' (which is what Facebook calls it) on EdgeRank?

The algorithm ranks 'weight' (relevance), 'affinity' (popularity) and 'time decay'. This latter one feels like a harsh comment on the timeliness of your news and posts but social media is a fast-paced world, and old news (which is anything older than the day before) is not looked at forgivingly.

EdgeRank looks at how often you post, the number of followers who read, Like or comment on your posts as well as your own track record on interaction. EdgeRank evaluates the comments or responses that your posts receive from your community of followers and fans.

You can help your EdgeRank scores by having a Facebook Like button on your site and blog. Here are some other ways to start creating a community that enjoys interacting with your business.

Using Facebook for your business:

1. Be interactive! Facebook is not meant to operate as a stream of facts or information. Ask for your fans' opinions, ideas, competition entries, helpful tips and so on and respond to those when they are posted.

2. Competitions and contests are an excellent way to encourage interaction. Make the prizes or services that you offer compelling and fun, and you can also ask people to post a comment on a blog or watch a related short video as an entry requirement.

3. You can also run contests on your website or on your offline advertising that encourage people to join your Facebook Page in exchange for entry into a prize draw or something similar. You can email your email list with a

link to your Facebook Page when you are in the process of starting your Page or growing it.

4. Consider giving an advance preview or an early introduction to new services or products to your Facebook Page first. Loyal fans will appreciate being given a preview or a special offer and are likely to spread the news.

5. If you use videos on Facebook (and you should!), do embed them from your YouTube channel rather than sending people away from your page to see the videos on YouTube itself.

6. You can also insert forms from customer relationship software like InfusionSoft directly onto your Facebook page to encourage sign ups to your newsletter or blog.

7. Welcome new visitors to your page with a special message and an invitation to 'Like' your page.

8. Post daily and respond daily. It makes a difference to the freshness of your content and people will likely miss a couple of your week's posts anyway amongst the flow of posts from their ever-growing circles of friends.

9. As a business owner, you may have long forgotten the concept of taking a weekend off, which is a good thing as far as your social media is concerned, because many more people tend to spend more time on Facebook at the weekends, so posting on a Saturday or Sunday can be a good strategy.

10. Do incorporate a gentle call to action on some posts. You could ask people to 'Like' a post if it strikes a chord with them, or to visit your site for an update or give them a reason to watch a new video you have posted. Fans are responsive as long as the overall quality of your posts and content is high and consistent.

11. By all means highlight your product or service, but elegance is the key. If you consider that 8 out of 10 posts should not be selling in any way shape or form, you will have a good rule of thumb. Those 8 posts should be helpful, fun and informative so that people are receptive to the other 2, sales-related posts. If you literally think of your fans as your friends, you will be on the right track. You wouldn't spend time with your friends and try and sell them on your new products the entire time; you might mention what you are working on or launching as part of a more inclusive, entertaining meeting. That is the same approach that will work best on Facebook and on social media networks as a whole.

12. Related to the point above is - have fun! Facebook is a relaxed haven where people go to enjoy their time. Nobody is on Facebook purely because it is informative (they have Wikipedia for that) or educational. They want to interact and have a good time, so without losing your innate professionalism and company ethos, it is a good idea to relax and entertain.

13. Brainstorm more interactive content. For instance, instead of posting a text interview or podcast, you can host an interview in the form of a live chat on your Wall with an expert in your field.

14. Don't forget to 'Like' other businesses' Facebook Pages. You have everything to gain with an abundance mentality and by sharing your approbation with companies you like or are interested in. You could start with the Pages of business partners, clients, suppliers and prospects. Facebook will notify the administrators of those Pages and some of them may Like your Page in return, exposing it to their Pages' fans.

15. Track your metrics. Facebook provides pages of

Insights that give you graphs and charts detailing how many people and what percentage are interacting with your Page and how often. Obviously you want this to be as high as possible.

You can look at any spikes in your gathering of 'Likes' and track that to particular marketing activities that you used at the time. Overall you will get a sense of what kinds of content are working best to engage your fans. You can also see 'unsubscribes' or people leaving your page. If you have spikes in this number, it is well worth tracking back to see what post or activities might have contributed to people turning away from your business.

Facebook has created a monolith that engages a phenomenal number of people. Leverage its branding and power to create more awareness and prospects for your business.

Linked In

LinkedIn is the social network most clearly associated with making connections in the business world, and it is based in part on the old saying, it's not what you know that counts, but who you know.

LinkedIn is a professional networking site designed specifically for professionals and business owners to connect with each other and share contacts and referrals. The profile you create on LinkedIn reads more like a CV or resume than other social media profiles. It includes your work history, your current position and it can include recommendations from those you have worked with in the past.

You can create a group or a page for your company as well as for yourself. All 500 of the Fortune 500 companies are represented on LinkedIn (and almost all at a high level of directors). It has become a business standard and it has almost 10 million members at the time of writing.

LinkedIn has some fences as a network. You cannot set up a profile and link to just anyone. You need to have a contact in common, or to have worked with someone, or have a personal relationship with a person, in order to initiate contact with a member. That member then needs to accept your request, and vice versa.

LinkedIn is mainly used for:

- Gaining referrals from the people who are connected to you
- Recommendations you may be seeking for a post you need to fill
- Showcasing yourself and your business as an outstanding product or service provider
- Networking in general
- Sharing advice and ideas within your industry or across complementary industries

As with any social network, creating a profile is not enough. You need to populate it with current and, ideally, continuously updated information, and then to also participate in discussions, groups and networks.

Using LinkedIn effectively:

1. A good place to start is by importing your address book. LinkedIn makes it easy to then contact those people in your list who are already on LinkedIn. Contacting friends, colleagues, previous business acquaintances and so on can provide a solid base to start your list of connections.

2. Nurture connections so that they are meaningful and useful relationships. According to Guy Kawasaki, users with more than 20 connections are 34 times more likely to receive job opportunities than those with fewer than 5 connections. LinkedIn creates a sense of trust - and people naturally prefer to work with those they trust.

3. Complete your profile. Go back and ensure your previous work history or previous companies are noted in your profile, as well as your college, university or school, as many people use LinkedIn to connect with old school or college friends. Also, an incomplete profile can leave people wondering if you are hiding something.

4. Definitely ensure that you have placed your business's URLs and email addresses into your profile.

5. You should also post a picture on your profile. Pictures draw people in much more effectively and, amongst a list of equally compelling profiles, the one with the head shot will usually get much more attention. Needless to say, the picture should be good quality and convey a good feeling about you. If you are a media company, you might not need to have a suit-and-tie type of headshot, but even a relaxed shot should be crisp, with good lighting and you should look approachable. Think as far away from a passport photo as possible.

6. Add a LinkedIn button to your email signature.

7. LinkedIn is a trusted site and so has a good Google Page Rank (as discussed in the SEO section, this is different from a search engine ranking and is related to a site's authority and link quality). You can make the most of this by ensuring your profile information is available for search engines to rank. There is an option in LinkedIn to do this by clicking 'Full View' in your public profile and you can customize your URL.

8. Link your profile to your business's Twitter stream and to your blog - you can do this through LinkedIn tools or through widgets.

9. LinkedIn has a reference check tool through which

you can find people who have worked with someone you might be considering hiring, or you can find out more about the person who is hiring you. In the same vein, before you attend an interview, you can find out more about the person who is interviewing you so that you can be aware of any common ground or similar interests.

10. You can use LinkedIn searches to gather information about any number of things, from which companies are shedding employees to which sectors are seeing more start ups than others. You can also initiate conversations with people who have experience that might be relevant to you as you start or grow your own business.

11. LinkedIn Answers lets you ask business-led questions to your network but also to the LinkedIn network as a whole. You should also try and answer questions that are asked, as long as you have something useful and insightful to offer.

12. Join groups related to your business's category, or to your wider business interests, or groups that are discussing ideas you are interested in pursuing in the future. It can be a good way to get a grass roots, insider look at things before you take your business down a certain path.

13. Use LinkedIn to do some research on prospects before you meet them. Finding common business links or interests can be very helpful and prospects will appreciate that you took the time to do your homework.

14. LinkedIn is a business and professional network - but, in common with your strategy on other social media platforms, that means you should not hard sell, or sell much at all.

15. That said, you can certainly request recommendations and testimonials, which is an accepted part of the LinkedIn structure, and you should be willing to do the same for

your contacts and to offer testimonials even when you have not been asked.

16. We have talked about holding interviews or guest content from professionals or experts in your field as a way to provide good content to your social media followers - LinkedIn is a great way to locate such experts and invite them to be interviewed, to speak at a conference or to provide a guest blog for your site.

17. LinkedIn has ads that can be finely targeted to your target market and ideal customers, particularly if you sell business to business products or services.

18. You can use LinkedIn to look for applicants for a vacancy you might have or to find suppliers who will come with recommendations and testimonials.

YouTube

There is an inherent power that moving images have to draw people in and make them connect. Previously, this was the domain of storytelling and movie-making, but now video rules the internet. The reason I haven't spent much time talking you through the nuts and bolts of setting up online accounts or using social media software is that a quick search on Google will bring up videos that will show you how to do things much more effectively than a traditional text-based manual.

About half of all online traffic is now videos. It is quick, convenient and often entertaining to watch. Online video used to be only for large companies with plenty of money to spend on professional crews, lighting, editing suites and bandwidth but thanks to a series of mini-revolutions in digital cameras, excellent built-in audio, and editing software, it has never been easier to create videos quickly.

YouTube is owned by Google, and is the second largest search engine. Video content drives traffic, creates awareness and excitement and can increase leads. It has this power primarily because video puts a face to your company and creates a visible, tangible sense of who you are, what you do and the kind of culture you believe in. Images give us incredible insight and we begin to trust and distrust based on a scan of someone's face and based on intuitions and insights that we can sometimes barely articulate.

Of course, these assets apply to any video site or post, not just to YouTube, but YouTube has grown to dominate our culture when we think of online video entertainment. There are many other sites that have wonderful aspects, but for the purposes of this book, I will focus on YouTube. Many of the ideas and tips that apply for YouTube will equally apply to other sites like Vimeo, Daily Motion and so on.

Through our film production arm, Enlightenment Productions, we experienced first hand the extraordinary viral power of YouTube. Our films 'I Can't Think Straight' and 'The World Unseen' were so popular and touched such a chord with audiences that a very niche, independent market mushroomed through word-of-mouth. Thousands of fans began to create their own videos using clips from the films, and to share them and to link from them. At the time of writing, YouTube clips related to these movies have over 100 million hits and counting.

Benefits of using video:

1. On the internet, where you can potentially interact with any stranger in any connected country, video allows you to give your business a face and a voice. It is the closest you can get to personally greeting each person who visits your website.

2. Videos are excellent for demonstrating the unique attributes of your product or service.

3. You can hold a seminar or host a discussion or broadcast an interview using video.

4. Video ranks high and well on search engines. You can choose to search for 'video only' results on Google and the other engines, but even in standard results, you will see video coming up more and more.

5. Following on from that point, video can be optimized well for internet searches and can be a big help in increasing your search engine rankings. At EBS Digital we offer a video SEO package as a stand alone product.

6. Video is easy to produce and relatively inexpensive. Today, good mobile phones have HD quality video recording, but even if you shoot with a small camera, the hardware and software you need to finish and edit the video is accessible and user-friendly. One of the services we can provide for our clients is video creation, and in a video-aware world, it is becoming more and more popular.

YouTube is an online network of video content that allows you, and encourages you, to upload, watch, rate, share and comment on videos. As a business, you can set up a channel that is customized with your logo and details and to which people can subscribe.

There are some phenomenal statistics about how widely used YouTube is, but the main point to note is how easy and simple they have made it to create, upload, market and stream video content, even for those of us, like me, who are not the most technical.

Using YouTube for your business:

1. Create a channel

Setting up a YouTube account is simple and if you have an existing Google account, you can use that to create your YouTube account.

Within YouTube, you then create a channel that your viewers can subscribe to. Try for a keyword-rich title that includes your line of business rather than just your company name, as this may help people searching for content and it can help associate your content with similarly-themed videos.

2. Customize your channel

YouTube allows you to change your channel page themes, colors and so on, and to upload images and your company logo or slogan. Take advantage of this to emphasize your branding and to make your channel look like an extension of your website.

3. Put contact information into videos

Not every video (and perhaps not any video) should be a sales pitch. A lot will be informational and entertaining or just introductory. That doesn't mean you should not include a link to your website or to specific product information in your video, usually towards the end. Make it easy for viewers to access your website when they have finished and are ready for more information.

4. Use annotations

YouTube allows you to overlay text boxes of different kinds throughout your videos, so that small captions can come up on the screen when you would like them to, with messages of your choice. Don't overuse annotations as they will distract from the main video, but towards the end they can be useful to give extra product information, or to reinforce your site URL or to direct people to your blog for more information on a certain topic and so on.

5. Embed videos

Once your video is uploaded to YouTube, you can embed the video in your website or blog and share it with your entire social media network. You can, of course, get a straightforward link to post up, but YouTube provides an embed code also (under the 'Share' button) which has the advantage of embedding the video within your site and keeping visitors there to watch it.

6. Link to YouTube

YouTube has a Google Page Rank of 9. The highest possible ranking is 10, and a 9 score is beyond the scope of most standard websites. A link from YouTube is therefore regarded as a very high quality link and will contribute to your site's overall ranking. Make sure that your account profile and your videos all link back to your website.

7. Use your channel to interact

People can leave comments on your channel page and they can also subscribe to you. Always reply to the comments and you can also send a bulletin to subscribers every now and then with news or a link to a related blog or topic.

8. Monitor comments beneath videos

Each video page has a section for comments. You can disable this if you wish, but it can be useful to create a dialogue between viewers and to receive feedback. You can remove or block any unwanted comments, but also use this section to respond to queries or curiosity. When we posted our film trailers and videos, people would often post questions about where they could buy the full movie, or which music we had used. Replying to these can bring you more customers.

9. Add video comments

In the same way that people comment on your videos, you can add your text comments to other videos you find useful. But you can also add a video comment and post a video of your own. Posting beneath popular videos gives your own video more visibility to a wider audience.

10. Optimize your video for search

Video content needs to be optimized for search results in a similar way to other content on your website. Here are some tips:

a. Use your keywords in the title of your video. Titles can be long, so take advantage of that, as it can help you be found more easily.

b. Put the video on a page that is relevant to the content of the video. The relevance of the page will contribute to the ranking of your video.

c. Take advantage of YouTube's description section to place more keywords and an appealing description of your video content. For instance, if it is a How To video, be specific about what your viewer can expect to learn.

d. YouTube also gives you plenty of space to add tags and extra keywords, and it will even suggest some for you. Use as many relevant tags as you can, as these all help for searches.

e. Make your videos good!

This perhaps sounds obvious, but your video will do well, and has the most chance of going viral if it is entertaining and holds attention well, because people will forward it, recommend it and link to it. There are a few aspects to video quality:

a. The actual picture quality. These days, it is hard to find a camera that takes poor images, so the crispness and definition of your video should be fine. Where people often take shortcuts is on light. You do not need a professional lighting kit, though if you plan to produce a series of interviews or something similar, a couple of well-chosen key and fill lights might be useful. But do make sure there is adequate lighting and stay away from harsh fluorescent lights which can make your video subject look washed out and unattractive. Just train yourself to look at the viewfinder critically. If it looks good in the viewfinder, it will probably look fine on the finished video.

b. Sound quality. As a film producer, I can't tell you how many times people view a movie with rough or unmixed sound and they think the picture is poor quality. Bad sound leaves a bad impression. Certainly, in this era of webinars and homemade videos, viewers make allowances for less than perfect audio, but if you can use an external mike for interviews or podcasts, your results will be crisper and more appealing.

Strategies

Blogging

In the previous section we discussed the use of blogging to help your search engine optimization, and that you should always have a blog on your website. It's an informal and fast-moving way to keep in touch with your clients and prospects.

Having and writing a blog is one aspect, but marketing it so that people are interested in your content and so that they begin to see you as the expert in your field, is another, even more important step.

The quality of the content is absolutely crucial and the look and presentation or frequency of your blogs can do very little to hide poor content. When I talk about content, I am not talking about grammar, punctuation or perfect phrasing. You do not have to be a great writer (or a technical wizard) to create a successful blog. What you do need is some insight or expertise or an opinion about a specific topic or idea.

If you really dislike writing or distrust your abilities, you may want to get someone in your company with a flair for putting words together to write your blog for you, or to outsource it altogether to a professional copywriter, or to a company like ours that produces dynamic blog content with reference to your wider marketing aims. But blogs are still a good opportunity for you to provide the background content and to position that content within your wider marketing strategy.

Benefits of Blogging:

1. Blogs help drive new and targeted traffic to your website

A blog allows you to create a fresh and constant supply of valuable content that markets your business and helps your SEO and online marketing. Well written blog posts also motivate their readers to click through to your site for more information. For this reason, you want your blogs to be information-rich but to leave certain questions unanswered or simply to intrigue the reader about the benefits you offer, so that they are motivated to click further.

2. Search engines love blogs

You know this by now, but providing fresh and keyword-rich content creates relevance and authority, two of the most important traits for search engine crawlers.

Although I highly recommend you keep your blog published on your site, and not solely on an external site, it is worth noting that search engines frequently crawl popular blog sites like Blogger and Wordpress, so it does no harm to copy your blog to some of those sites as well. You may reach an audience outside your current website and social network circles.

3. Blogs can position you and your company as experts

Your positioning helps towards building your brand and to deciding how people will begin to perceive your brand. Online publishing builds authority and credibility, even if it is just through blogs to begin with. When your prospects and customers read and learn to trust what you have to say, you will have built a following of potential customers.

Blogging for your business:

1. Focus each blog on a single topic or theme, even if you are examining many aspects of it. For instance, rather than writing a blog about internet marketing as a topic, I may be better off focusing on '10 ways to market your website' or '3 things to look out for when building an e-store'. This helps people find you when they are looking for answers about the specific issue you are discussing, and it draws on your expertise. Many people know a broad amount about internet marketing, but they might not know some of the tips on very specific issues.

2. Choose topics you know well or that you can source interesting information about. Readers will already have an interest in your topic and will quickly pick up inaccuracies.

3. Brainstorm 20 or 30 possible topics that stem from your niche market and the extraordinary value you provide to customers. Also think about news topics related to your

industry, a question a customer had, frequently asked questions about your business and industry, or personal stories that relate to your topic. You will feel better just having a list and one idea often leads to another and another.

4. Think about behind-the-scenes information that might be interesting. Is there a way that you manufacture a product that would surprise people, or that would reinforce the intrinsic quality of your products? When we produced our feature films, viewers loved short, behind-the-scenes clips where they could see our lead actresses relaxed and off duty.

5. Don't restrict yourself to your products and services - if you are a builder, you can discuss frequent problems that people find when they renovate their homes and how to avoid them.

6. If you have the time, you can research the topics you choose to see what people are already commenting on, what gaps there are in the information around that topic and to check whether your topic is highly competitive or not. Sites like Technorati, Google Trends and Google Blogsearch are all useful for this.

7. Look for unique perspectives based on your passions. If a builder cares about the environment, he could put a spin on his post that looks at how to build your home to be more environmentally friendly. If you serve a community in a cold weather region, how to weather-proof and save money could work as an angle that puts a new spin on building tips. Another example: at EBS Digital, we often work with female business owners - and the unique challenges and perspectives of being a woman in the marketing world could be an interesting angle for a blog we might do.

8. Be persistent and consistent. Some weeks it will feel as if no-one is listening or commenting. If you keep in mind

a goal of getting, say, 10 comments per blog post, it will keep you focused and you will begin to notice why some posts attract more comments than others, and that simple awareness will improve your blog writing.

9 .Use the header or title of your blog well. The headline should ideally contain a keyword and should get people interested in reading your content. For instance, using the example about our female business owners, rather than titling a blog 'Online marketing for female business owners' I might try '8 Ways Women Entrepreneurs Can Benefit Most From Online Marketing' or 'Why Online Marketing Really is Different If You Are a Female Business Owner'.

10. Use a small picture to illustrate your article or blog if you can. Visuals are always interesting for people.

11. You should use links in your blogs, as long as they are relevant - back to other pages on your site that have more information about a service you may be referencing, or to other companies or related sites. Conversely, if you can get an article posted on a website with a high page rank, that will help your own site's page rank. Blogs and articles are powerful link building strategies.

12. Use categories and tags - when you post your blog, you can add categories or tags to indicate to readers and search engines what the main topics and themes of your blogs are.

13. Consider adding a search box so that users can search for particular topics and find them easily in past blogs you have written.

14. Steer clear of walls of text - people are busy and they are bombarded with content today and many internet users skim blogs for the main points. Try to use bullet points,

images, short paragraphs, headlines and sub headlines to break up your text and keep the spacing overall at 1.5 lines wide so that it is even easier to read.

15. Get to your point quickly. Rambling is not a good idea in a blog. Lay out your topic or premise, why you chose it and why you think you can add to it, and then get straight to the meat of the blog or article.

16. Keep your writing simple and clear. If you are a good writer with an exceptional vocabulary, a blog might not be the best place to show that off, unless you are marketing yourself as a literary novelist. That doesn't mean you should not use your writing ability to create a good persona and personality for yourself. It might be witty, acerbic, friendly or as you please, but a sense of the character behind the blog helps people to connect to it.

17. Read other people's blogs. This is a good habit to get into, not just for technique tips but also to keep up with developments and ideas that are of interest to you in your industry and personally. I've mentioned Flipboard before, and apps like this make reading blogs and keeping up with your social media an absolute pleasure.

Promoting Your Blog:

Now that you have written your blog, you want people to find it.

1. Post a link to the blog on all your social media networks, keeping the title visible so that people who are interested can link back to your site for more.

2. Reply promptly to any comments you get.

3. Set up an RSS feed for your blog so that people can subscribe to it.

4. Leave good comments on other people's blogs. Generally you need to enter your name and website when you comment so that creates a useful link back to your site and ideally, to your own blog page. Try to make sure you have something useful or insightful to add to blog comments because that in itself will encourage people to want to know more about you.

5. Be generous about linking out. Successful social media happens from an abundance mentality. Giving links or a good review to content you have enjoyed takes nothing away from you and in fact, exposes good content to your followers and they will appreciate that you are filtering some of the torrent of internet content and passing on the gems. Connecting to other blogs and sites also encourages reciprocal links and dialogue within the blogging community.

6. Once you have a relationship with some other bloggers, you can ask them to write a guest post, which will also attract some of their own audience to your site. You can also ask other people in related industries, or with interesting stories related to your business to write a guest blog for you.

Articles

Quite a lot of the tips for good blogging apply to writing articles so I will not repeat those here.

You may wonder why you need to write articles at all if you are blogging regularly. Articles reach a different audience and there are a whole different set of directories for article posts so articles can have an extra impact on your website traffic and authority.

How to lay out an article:

As with almost everything to do with internet content, there are few hard and fast rules but you have a little more scope with article content than with blogs because they tend to be more wide-ranging (though still relating back to your business eventually). Your articles should always use some of your keywords though, as their likely appeal to your ideal clients is the primary reason you are writing them. You should have lists of keywords from your SEO activity that will be perfect to seed into articles.

The overall layout of your articles should use the marketing equation of:

Interrupt + Engage + Educate + Offer

Interrupt:

The headline or title of your article is what people will see when they are on the page where it sits, but it is also what they should see in search engine results, so make sure it is gripping enough to gain clicks from users.

Your USP might come in useful here, but you will need many more headlines as you build up a stock of articles. Good headlines can come from:

a. the unique benefits your business offers
b. FAQs
c. the biggest wants of your ideal customers

Headlines should also contain a keyword or two because if your article comes up and it clearly correlates with the search term used, people are more likely to click on it.

Engage/Educate:

The main part of your article should touch on your understanding of your readers' predicaments and engage them with some solutions and the suggestion of even more. It should do this by offering useful and good advice and expert information about the topics you outlined in your headline.

You do not need to answer every possible question they could have about a topic. You want them to come to your site, or to you directly, for more. It is an article, not a perfect solution, and the key is to give enough information so that your readers feel that you do know how to solve the problems or frustrations that led them to read your article in the first place.

Offer:

Your articles should always end with a strong call to action. This is not necessarily a sales pitch but simply a call to visit your website for more information. That is what drives traffic to your site from articles.

Be clear on what further solutions or ideas readers might be able to get from your website, and tell them where to find it, or link directly to the relevant page. Pages on your site that have a good offer of a free report or even a newsletter can be a good destination to direct people to. Using the builder as an example, it is more compelling to end an article with an offer of more information in the same vein, like a free report about 'How to insulate your home for winter'.

More tips for writing articles:

1. Keep articles relatively short and no more than 1000 words. Usually around 500 words works well. In the online world, people consume content quickly and in short bites.

2. As with blogs, bullet points and clear points work well.

3. Publish articles regularly. Weekly is wonderful, but even an article once a month provides a steady flow of new content for your followers and for the search engines.

4. Submit your articles to article directories. Examples are Ezine Articles. Your article can be browsed and even republished elsewhere. Your article will also always include a note at the bottom with your bio or details and your website address, which means that if your article is syndicated on other sites, you will get links back to your website from those sites.

5. Put your articles on social content sites like Squidoo. You can also add pictures and videos to Squidoo and members comment and interact and share content. If you want to try this strategy, you should make yourself an active member of the community as well. Social content sites, and social media overall, work best when there is give and take, not just a stream of content from you to your followers.

6. You can also contact related sites which might be interested in an article you have written and offer it to them. Content should obviously be relevant. Our builder might approach some construction trade suppliers or environmentally concerned sites if he has an energy-saving slant in his article.

7. Writing a good article takes a little work, so use parts of it in blogs, in tweets and in your email marketing. If the content is good, there is no reason not to use it in different ways.

8. Tell people about your article - you can email your

subscribers from your site, and post a link with the headline of your article across your social media profiles.

Podcasts & Videos

Podcasts are mostly associated with audio recordings, although they can be video as well, and they usually have the sense of being part of a series of broadcasts , very much like a blog that is audio and visual rather than written.

Generally, they are distributed as downloads through feeds that listeners can then listen to at their leisure.

You can give out all of the same information you would give in a blog in a podcast, and if you have someone you can chat with about the topics you are covering, it can create a good back and forth, interview and discussion-style program that is entertaining for your listeners.

Benefits of podcasts:

1. You can do product demos, or 'how to' explanations more easily with an audio or video cast.

2. You can run a series of courses.

3. Podcasts can be a good substitute for a written blog every now and then.

4. Podcasts can get your material out to a new audience of people who might prefer to listen to content on iPods or in their cars.

You can make a podcast using your computer's basic audio recording equipment. Garage Band on Mac is a great program for recording audio, and there are numerous apps which allow you to record content directly onto your cell phone and upload it to the internet.

Podcasts can be distributed through the major channels we have discussed. They should be posted on your site or embedded onto it, and in addition you can distribute podcasts through iTunes, through podcast channels such as Podcastalley.com, and by listing podcasts through directories like the aptly-named Podcastdirectory.com

Creating Videos:

Making your first video might seem slightly daunting, but having a clear outcome is a help and a good start.

1. Decide the purpose for your video. Do you want to position your business and yourself as an expert? Do you want to entertain or amuse and create a fun personality for your business? Do you want to show people how to use your products in different ways?

2. Based on your outcome, write down a brief outline of how you see the video in your mind. Is it a quick product demonstration in a workshop? An interview between two experts? An overview of your services?

3. This will lead into the third step which is to detail your outline into a script. Even if you envision a degree of ad libbing, you should create a script that gives you a reminder of what you want to say. This keeps your video from rambling, which will only lead people to turn it off.

4. Rewrite the script! Often your words will sound less natural when you read them aloud, so do that a few times and simplify your phrasing wherever possible.

5. If you are recording yourself on camera, don't be afraid to keep the video simple and clear. Your key message is the main element.

6. Use plenty of expression in your voice and face, without being excessive. If your video is all about you, you want to capture interest in your audience.

7. If you can't memorize your script and have to deliver lines to the camera, you can read a cue from the side, but you might also be able to creatively cut between lines to product lines or slides which reinforce your words with text bullet points.

8. Do keep some distance between you and your chosen background. This will look less 'flat' than standing right up against a wall or shelves behind you.

Equipment for Creating Videos:

- An HD camera. These are not hard to find, even on cell phones, but a compact, easy to use digital camera is the obvious first requirement.
- A tripod. This is more essential than you may realize, because no matter how still you think you are holding a camera, there is almost always some shake. Unless that is part of your vision for your video, steady your camera with a tripod for more professional results.
- A microphone. Built in microphones have become better and better but a mic that plugs into the camera sounds better. If you are doing a piece to camera or an interview, use a lapel mic with a long lead, and if you are doing a voiceover for a slideshow or narrating over your finished video, a mic that plugs into your computer's USB or audio input will work well.
- Editing software. Many computers today come with basic editing software. For Apple, it's iMovie. Adobe Premiere is also good, but the high end standard is Final Cut, which comes in a Pro version which can be used for anything including major feature films, and in an Express version which is smaller to run and use. These softwares have an impressive array of features from movie-quality transitions, to excellent graphics and color correction. If you are not excited about learning how to use a whole editing software then you

can always hire an editor or a student editor to work with you in finishing your videos. Our expertise and experience in editing features and promo videos mean we offer this service quickly and cost-effectively for companies requiring editing.

• Lighting equipment is not essential but a small, basic set of lights can make your video look much more professional and attractive.

If all this has filled you with dread, you can still create excellent video content without using a camera at all.

Powerpoint and Keynote are presentation softwares that allow you to easily put together slides of text and images. You can export these as movies at the click of a button.

You will want to add some audio to them, and I have used Keynote before to play through a presentation while recording audio into my computer. Keynote will then export the video with the audio overlaid, and with the slides moving forward at exactly the speed you chose.

If you want to use this method for creating multiple videos, try to use a mixture of text, ideally in bullets that briefly recap what you are saying in the voiceover, and also use images. There are free sites for images, but you should check that you have the right to use them on promotional video content. Otherwise sites like iStockPhoto have a vast selection of pictures at very reasonable prices.

Also, keep your slides moving forward briskly. In a webinar, you can get away with chatting over a slide for a few minutes or more, but in a short video, the screen should change regularly to reduce the chance of your viewers clicking away.

Video sharing sites

We have looked in detail at YouTube, but there are many, many well known and smaller video hosting sites on the internet.

Like posting your articles to directories, it can only be helpful to have your videos on channels on as many of these sites as possible. Uploading every video to 20 or 50 sites is time-consuming and takes time. There are systems that can help with this process - one example is OneLoad.

Once you have created channels or accounts with the major video services like Vimeo, Daily Motion and YouTube, you enter your log in information on OneLoad and it uploads your video to the different video sharing sites. This way, you click to upload once, but your content gets the wide distribution that can gain you more audiences.

They also have analytics that show you which sites are getting the most views for which videos. Along with Google Analytics, this forms a good base for you to see which videos work best and which are driving the most traffic to your site.

Online Press Releases & Public Relations

Many small businesses ignore PR (Public Relations) as a marketing strategy. Writing and sending out press releases used to be associated with expensive advertising and public relations firms, but this does not have to be the case any more.

Benefits of PR:

- Online PR applies to social media, blogs, social bookmarking and video sites and press release sites, so there is potential to garner a large audience
- Press releases are designed to be released and written up as editorial content and so have an inherent sense of being trustworthy and vetted, versus direct advertising. If you run an ad and see a newspaper story, and both have the same headline, the majority of us will believe the newspaper story over the ad.

- You do not pay for editorial coverage as you do for advertising.
- Even without editorial coverage, online distribution for your press releases can create interest, traffic and back links.

There are two main ways to approach online PR and which one you choose will be determined by your ultimate aims.

If you want to simply put out regular releases to announce new products, to embed keywords and help your SEO rankings, there is a system to that, similar to the one we follow when we do SEO for clients at EBS Digital.

If you want to get proper coverage in online newspapers, journals or TV sites, there is rather more work to be done. Let's look at this option first.

Getting stories into the media:

1. Do you have news to share? Every business does have news, but whether it matters outside the confines of your target market is the question.

2. Start a file for news story ideas and brainstorm every week on angles to pitch. Let loose with ideas as they can always be discarded but the more you brainstorm, the more you will come up with.

3. Once you have a starter list of ideas, think about them from the perspective of the audience of the media outlet you are targeting and from the editor of that outlet. Will they think it is as newsworthy as you do?

4. Once you have established a good news story, establish your angle. This should be a unique perspective. At a time when homeowners face dropping equity and foreclosure, perhaps your construction company has found a new way to improve home values. This example taps into a current

event (the recession and housing crash) and current events are always a good angle to work from as it will help your story feel timely to editors and journalists.

5. Many magazines and newspapers make information about their editorial calendars public. Do some research and you may be able to tailor your pitch around an upcoming story or feature.

When you pitch a story, give the journalist everything they need, including background, access to pictures, videos and so on. Make it as easy as you can for them.

6. If your news is truly important or mainstream or groundbreaking, you should consider hiring a PR firm or consultant to help craft and distribute your release. In the face of intense amounts of competition for coverage in the best known and most read news sources, a professional with contacts and expertise can help you get noticed and read by editors.

Writing Press Releases for general online marketing purposes:

If you would like to use press releases to distribute your content more widely, and to boost your SEO efforts, the same basic rules apply as for blogs, articles and your general web content - be authentic, be useful and informative with your content and do not generate poorly written releases for the sake of it.

A number of online press release distribution services offer writing or editing assistance as part of your distribution package but the help can be generic, though they can be helpful in giving you a basic format, which I will outline below.

A release once a month is often enough for standard press releases that deal with company updates, new products or similar news. If you send releases more frequently, you can get ignored, and your news will probably become less and less newsworthy with time as you scramble for interesting angles.

The best way to optimize is to write for people first and engines second, just as you need to do for all other content. You can then go back and place in some keywords that work naturally. Your keywords should link to the relevant page of your website (not necessarily the home page).

Press Release Layouts:

The rule of thumb is to place your most important content and concept at the start and work down into more detail.

There are certain accepted requirements when you create a press release:

1. The (current) date and the words 'For Immediate Release' or similar.

2. A headline. This should summarize the story and make the reader want to continue. Using our previous example: 'Boston construction firm finds boom in a housing bust' might work well. If you can place a keyword in there (like 'Boston construction'), that also helps.

3. The location - where is this news happening? A new product launch would be located at your business's main headquarters.

4. A short opening paragraph that summarizes the journalistic holy grail of 'who, what, where, when and how'. If, like a good elevator pitch, your headline created a question in the minds of the reader ('How did they do that?') then this paragraph should answer that question cleanly and clearly. Throughout your release, the more you can mimic the style of the outlets you would like it to reach, the easier you make it for journalists to use it without changing very much of your copy.

5. Evidence to back up your news - if you can add in

quotes, examples or photos that prove you did get the award you are writing about, that helps journalists to take your story seriously without needing to do immense research. Quotes are always a good idea as news stories like to use them. Quotes that double up as testimonials are even better.

6. Try to keep the main part of the release to 750 words or less.

7. Media contacts - details of who to call or email for follow-ups are essential.

8. A short bio or details of your company and what it offers, and details about the person involved in the news should be added at the very end, together with full contact details and your company's website.

9. Do not advertise. Press releases are promotional tools, but a good release should read like a news story, not an ad.

10. Use good grammar and check spellings. Releases with errors look as unprofessional as a resume with similar mistakes.

11. Stay away from using 'us', 'we' or 'you'. This is where press releases differ greatly from blogs. Releases are more formal in general.

Distributing Press Releases Online:

PRWeb is an online distribution service that sends your releases to subscribers, to major newswires and to search engines. There are other services such as PR.com, iNewswire and Pressbox that are also excellent, but PRWeb is perhaps the best known.

You can set up a free account and you can distribute to social media outlets, for SEO or to the major news sites. You can also add pictures and videos to the text releases that you upload and, like most such sites, PRWeb has a wide range of analytics for you to track how many times your release has been read and how often the links within it are clicked.

Managing Your Social Media

You may be wondering how you can fit in all of this social media activity and still have time left over to actually run your business.

Well, the idea is that, if it is done well and consistently, your social media efforts should take your leads, sales and business to the next level, so it is worth some of your time. It will require some scheduling and discipline to make it work, especially because many social media networks (like Twitter) thrive on immediacy.

Start a Content Calendar

A content calendar is a good way to organize all the ideas you have created from brainstorming and it helps you to decide whether your content is good or just filler.

Start out with a longer term calendar for your business highlights, showing new product launches, new services, anniversaries, awards or other special events. This is a good base from which to plan out press releases, newsletters and so on.

Add an Editorial Calendar

In addition, you can set up a one month calendar which structures your daily and weekly posts across your business's social media sites.

This should literally map out each day's proposed content for each site. For instance, if you blog on a Friday, that blog might be linked to across all your sites, but on the same day you might add a couple of other Twitter posts. You would decide and write into the calendar what those tweets might be, whether they involve posting a photo, or a link to a video, or an external article.

Schedule Your Time

To avoid being constantly on social media sites, try to set aside twenty minutes in the morning and twenty in the evening, plus some time for content production. Or a few minutes every hour might suit you. You can decide and allocate more or less time according to what works best and your degree of involvement.

Use Apps to Keep Track

There are many apps that work by taking in RSS feeds and that let you bring together many of your social media accounts under one umbrella. Using apps like this help you to keep track of your posts and the responses of your followers without logging into several different accounts.

Outsource Social Media

You can, of course, assign some of the social media updates to someone else in your organization.

You can also outsource entirely to an online marketing company, but you need to be sure they understand your goals, your company culture and how to produce quality content.

These last three points are central to our social media marketing at EBS Digital. It is one of the reasons we tend not to provide set packages for social media, but we always customize our proposals to suit the growth and strategy of each individual business.

Final Analysis

You are an entrepreneur, or a business owner, or someone who runs a business or who is deeply interested in the marketing of a business. The online world offers immense opportunity for your business in ways that none of us could have dreamed of just a few years ago.

If you want to supply someone in the Far East from your business location in the middle of the USA, the opportunity is there and vice versa. With digital delivery, you can supply those products forever with a small set up cost and with virtually no operational costs at all.

If you have struggled to make a dent against larger and more established corporations, you can spend just a little time defining the psychographics of your ideal client, choosing a niche market that serves a specific issue they have, and then innovating your business so that you no longer compete, but you create.

Entrepreneurs often have a unique perspective. They usually have tenacity, courage, vision and a way of looking at failures as learning processes that will help them make the next success come a little more easily. It is not an easy road to choose, but you choose to run a business because it offers rewards.

As human beings we are at our best and most expressive when we can create. Serving customers and clients in ways that bring them extraordinary value, producing systems and products that are exceptional, thinking of ways to make our businesses stand out - these are all creative acts.

Creation is entirely different from competition.

Often, we are brought up to be competitive - with our classmates for grades and prizes, with co-workers, with siblings, with other businesses in our field. It is a great thing to strive for greatness, but someone else's success takes nothing away from our success, and the ultimate goal is to create in our lives and our businesses, and not to compete.

Good marketing, and the use of online marketing, has made that level of creation much more achievable for anyone starting out in business today. Online marketing and social media encourage and reward creativity in your business thinking.

The trials and tribulations, the challenges and disasters still come, and there will always be a fundamental need for integrity and high standards of products and services. But there has been a leveling of the playing field - someone with no money to rent a brick and mortar store can set up a shop online through portals like ebay, with no outlay except, possibly, for stock.

Online marketing makes it possible for any site to drive traffic to view its offerings using SEO and PPC. These are huge strides, and immense opportunities and it is these opportunities that inspired me to start EBS Digital with the mission of helping small and medium sized businesses find their niche and expand into it. We have also tried to put into practice the philosophy of adding extra value. We recognized that many businesses have tried SEO and online marketing without getting the results they had expected or wanted. And often, that was because SEO companies often just did some basic keyword analysis and then, with varying success, implemented the technical requirements for sending websites slowly up the search engine rankings.

This turned out to be insufficient - because there is usually no help from SEO companies to laser target prospects who **want** your services rather than everyone who might **need** them. There is no help to craft a marketing message that compels people to take action. And there is no help for you to adjust your website structure, focus and design to effectively capture data and offer exceptional value.

With EBS Digital, we wanted to make all these marketing fundamentals, and more, a part of a more holistic process to drive traffic to your site. Nobody knows your business better than you do, and for this reason, you are the best person to decide who to market to and how to market to them - but you may not have all the tools and skills and resources you need to do that. Creating our membership site at www.ebsdigitaluniversity.com was our way of pooling all these resources into one central place where business owners can go to access everything they need to make their sales and marketing expand beyond their previous dreams. The site stands alone as a paid membership facility but by making it available for free to all of our SEO customers, we found a way to add exceptional value to business owners.

I hope that this book has helped to open up some of the possibilities and potential of marketing online and offline, and I'd like to thank you for taking the time to read it. If you have any questions about what we do at EBS Digital, or if you want to find out if we can help you, feel free to email me at hanan@ebsdigital.com.

Finally, because you clearly care deeply about the success of your business, I would like to offer you an in depth analysis of your website. Running to over 8 pages, this assessment will leave you with a very clear picture of your site's health in terms of search engine friendliness and user compatibility. We generally charge $499 for it, but as a thank you for buying this book, we would like to offer it to you free of charge. Just email my team at advice@ ebsdigital.com, quoting the 'Grow Your Profits' offer and providing us with your business URL, and we will get the analysis prepared for you.

If you enjoyed my book, I would appreciate you taking a few minutes to review Grow Your Profits on Amazon. co.uk and Amazon.com.

You can also follow me on Twitter at HananKattanEBS

Below is a short list of books that I have enjoyed and that have made a difference in my life:

The Master Key System - Charles F. Haanel

The Science of Being Rich - Wallace D. Wattles

Think and Grow Rich - Napoleon Hill

Rich Dad, Poor Dad - Robert Kiyosaki

The Seven Habits of Highly Effective People - Stephen Covey

The Road Less Travelled - M Scott Peck